Your Towns and Cities in the C

C000079775

Romford

in the Great War

Your Towns and Cities in the Great War

Romford

in the Great War

by Stephen Wynn

Pen & Sword
MILITARY

First published in Great Britain in 2016 by
PEN & SWORD MILITARY
an imprint of
Pen and Sword Books Ltd
47 Church Street
Barnsley
South Yorkshire S70 2AS

ISBN 978 1 47382 2 207

A CIP record for this book is available from the British Library

Printed and bound in England
by CPI Group (UK) Ltd, Croydon, CR0 4YY

Pen & Sword Books Ltd incorporates the imprints of
Pen & Sword Archaeology, Atlas, Aviation, Battleground, Discovery,
Family History, History, Maritime, Military, Naval, Politics, Railways,
Select, Social History, Transport, True Crime, and Claymore Press,
Frontline Books, Leo Cooper, Praetorian Press, Remember When,
Seaforth Publishing and Wharncliffe.

For a complete list of Pen and Sword titles please contact
Pen and Sword Books Limited
47 Church Street, Barnsley, South Yorkshire, S70 2AS, England
E-mail: enquiries@pen-and-sword.co.uk
Website: www.pen-and-sword.co.uk

Contents

Preface

What I have tried to achieve in this book is to provide the reader with a flavour of what life was like throughout the Romford, Hornchurch and Upminster areas during the First World War and how those who lived and worked there were affected, both on the home front and by having loved ones fighting overseas.

Although every effort has been made to record all of the war memorials and church-based rolls of honour throughout the district, we accept it is almost inevitable that we have missed at least one. If we have, then we apologize.

It is hoped in writing this book that we have provided you the reader with a flavour of the history of the local district, the mayhem and bloodshed of the First World War, as well as the heroism and the fortitude of the soldiers and families involved.

The war brought with it social change on a scale and at a pace which had never been seen before. These were ground-breaking times that there would be no going back on. For some, the war was a way out of a life of drudgery and desperation, to a world of adventure and excitement, but many would end up paying a terrible price for their new freedoms and way of life.

Was it worth it? Were any lessons learnt? Did the end justify the means? Read through the following pages and decide for yourself. Maybe it will encourage you to research your own family and relatives in greater detail, either those who lived through the war on the home front, or the young men who were in the armed forces involved in the actual fighting.

Acknowledgements

Stephen would like to say thank you to his wife Tanya for her continued support and encouragement.

Stuart Lynch for the photographs of the Hornchurch War Memorial, and Sean Connolly for the photographs of the War Memorials and Rolls of Honour throughout the Romford area, as well as for the rest of the help he provided for this book.

CHAPTER 1

A Brief History of Romford

The Romford district has a long history, with Roman artefacts having been discovered in the areas of Collier Row, Noak Hill and Harold Hill. The town is first recorded in 1177 and is initially referred to as Romfort, the name believed to be taken from the Old English of 'rum' and 'ford', meaning 'the wide or spacious ford'.

The town has had its own market square since 1247, this giving it a certain social status. Romford's early history is one of agriculture with the area having a number of flour mills for the grinding of corn.

For nearly four hundred years from the fifteenth to the early nineteenth centuries, the area of Romford had a very large leather industry. Other industries included cloth making, brewing and weaving, to name but a few.

It was a relatively small town until the start of the eighteenth century when it became a coaching town. Even then the population grew to no more than just a few thousand people, living in approximately 500 homes.

The railway came to Romford in 1839 on the Eastern Counties Railway services out of London. This developed the economy and caused a considerable growth in population. Romford acquired a second railway station in 1892 which ran on the London to Southend line giving it a direct link to Tilbury Docks.

The Local Government Act of 1894 created the Romford Urban District and the Romford Rural District and in the following years economic growth continued, particularly between 1910 and 1911 with the construction of Gidea Park Garden Suburb, which included Raphael Park as well as a railway station for the area.

Just after the end of the First World War, the 1921 census showed the population of Romford to be 19,442. It has continued to rise steadily ever since, although there have been significant boundary changes since then.

CHAPTER 2

Romford War Memorial

The Romford Memorial was unveiled in 1921 in Laurie Square in the town centre but it was moved to its current location at Coronation Gardens in 1969 to make way for the town's new ring road.

This wasn't uncommon up and down the country over the course of time. Many of the old towns that have war memorials were little more than village communities back in the early 1920s when most of the memorials were originally erected. As these communities grew, so did their need to build more properties and roads, which resulted in war memorials having to be relocated.

There are the names of 360 young men commemorated on the Romford War Memorial:

(Photograph by Sean Connolly)

E W Adams	S F Adams	J J Ager
R G Alabaster	S P Allam	C Archer
G Ault	H W Austin	H S Baldwin
C H Ball	E J Barber	A P Barford
A E Barker	G Barker	S R Bently
A M Besant	A W Biggs	C S Biggs
B C Biner	J A Bishop	J W Bishop
W Bixby	H F Blackwell	H Booth
H Booth	L J Booty	A Rowley
A W Bragg	G J Bragg	S Bragg
S D Bramble	W J Branson	J H Brightwell
C Brooks	H Brooks	H J Brooks
F R Broom	E D Brown	H Brown
S Broyd	H W Bryant	C H Bugbee
G Buggs	F J Bush	G Bush
J A Butterworth	B A Campling	C O P Carter
E N Carter	C H Cast	F Castle
A E Chambers	H J Chambers	J J Chandler
C J Chopping	G F Clark	H Climson
W Collard	S V Cook	H L Cooke
A J Cooper	L J Cooper	P L Cormack
R O Cormack	R H Courtney	T A Cox
R Crudgington	C Cumberland	C R F Davis
F J Day	W A Dean	G Denton
H W Digby	W Disney	W Dole
A Dorrington	C L Dowsett	H Drew
C J Eary	J Eggleton	R C Eley
A Ellingworth	H Ellis	H E Everitt
E Felstead	R W Finch	S G Finch
T Finch	G A J Flack	W E Flight
F I Forster	A D Fox	E V French
C R Gardener	W J Gardner	W O Garnett
L H Garnham	W George	F Coke
A Gooding	H Gosling	W Gowers

S Grantham	J Green	L V De L Grogan
H W Guiver	F Hale	H W Hale
D Haley	H Hall	T B Hammond
A Hanson	A H Harding	C W Harding
F F Hardingham	L Hards	W Hardy
A J Harper	J E Harrington	J Hasler
G Hawkins	W Hawkins	D Haynes
W T Hearn	A Hillbourne	A Hills
H G Hills	H Hilton	H P Hitch
C E Holby	R Hollick	T G Holmes
W J Horsman	J A J Horsnail	S T Hotson
T L Howe	W J Howe	E W Hoy
R L Hughes	F J Humphreys	G Isbell
F G Jackson	C Jennings	C Johnson
A E Jones	H E Jones	H Kelly
J F Kewley	A King	E King
J F Kiy	A Knight	P Kronenberger
C W Lambert	F J Langstone	H W Langstone
W B Lasham	D J Laundy	E W Laundy
S J Laundy	A F Hazell	W H Leach
H Leggatt	W Leggatt	T Letton
G Lewis	C Linsell	F Linsell
F J Linsell	F Locke	W Lovegrove
A A Lynch	B T Major	H Marden
P J Marden	A E Marsh	A T Matthews
S T Matthews	H W Mawer	A Mayes
A J Mayes	F W Meekings	F A Meggy
W Meloy	A V Metson	S Michell
J Millbourne	F W Miller	S A Millett
A F Milton	A R Moore	K W J Moore
T W Moss	J C Mullett	R G Murphy
W R New	A V Newlin	F Norman
E Nunn	W J Nunn	C F Osman
S E Ottley	W E Owen	H Palmer

J R Palmer	S D Parker	A F Partridge
H Pasfield	J Pasfield	W Pasfield
A Pasterfield	H A Patience	J E Payne
G Peacock	F Pead	G Pead
C W Pegrum	G W Perry	R H Perry
R J Perry	S R J Perry	W Perry
B J Pewter	A J Pharoah	C E Phillips
J B Phillips	W H Phillips	F J Pond
F Ponder	H S Poole	C Pope
C J Popplewell	C G Porter	G H Potter
J Potter	D W Prentice	B S Prior
R C Prior	B W Pye	R Ramsey
F H Randall	F Rayment	H J Raymond
E Reeve	A G Rich	R Richman
W T J Rivers	W S Roberts	S Robison
A A Rogers	A H Rogers	W E Rose
J Rowlett	B G Ruffle	J P Runacres
R J Rushen	A Saggers	A A Saggers
C A Sams	E V Sandwell	W H Sanford
H A Saunders	S E Saunders	A Savill
A Scott	W Scott	H Seyd
J H Seymour	J J Sharp	G J Shaw
J Shearman	C H Shelley	H Shorthose
J Siggins	C W Simmons	L W Skilton
T Small	H V Smart	S Smith
W J Smith	W T Spriggs	H W Spingett
E Staff	F Staff	A G Staines
C B Stalley	W A Starr	R N Stevens
R Stone	W Stone	E J Stuart
E S Such	J H Such	W H Surridge
H Swallow	F A Tattersall	F C Taylor
F J Taylor	L Taylor	S R H Taylor
F C Theobald	J McD Thomson	W Thomson
E V Thurgood	B Thurgood	E Tite

F Tite	H Took	W C Took
H T Trotman	J H Turner	L G Turner
W J Turner	T Twaits	W A G Tyrrell
A J Vale	C W Vine	F Walden
J Want	G H Warman	P A Warman
A S Warren	G Weavers	H T Webb
W C A Webb	W W Webb	C T H Weedon
F C Wells	L M Wells	W R Wells
W O Westrop	A J Weal	F O Wheatley
E Whipps	J Whitaker	J Whitrod
E Wiffen	W T B Wilson	G Wilson
F Wilkinson	L E Winch	C W Wood
E Wood	H Wood	J A Wood
H W Wooler	G F Wooley	A Wopling
O S Wraight	W A Wraight	E A Wright
F H Wright	R R Wright	C W C Young
H W Young	R C Young	H G Bannister

Many of these names are also recorded on some of the District's other war memorials and church rolls of honour. This came about in the main as there were no official criteria set down as to how an individual's name was included on a particular memorial. This unsurprisingly led to both duplication and omissions.

There are so many names recorded on the Romford War Memorial that it is regrettably impossible to look at every one of them in this book, although each of their stories is just as valuable and important

Unveiling of Romford War Memorial.
(Romford, Collier Row & Gidea Park – Phillimore Brian Evans)

as all the rest. I will, however, look at a small selection of them in some detail.

The name **Pasfield** appears on the memorial three times. John and William Pasfield were brothers and along with their parents, William and Mary Pasfield, their brother Edward and their five sisters, they lived at number 81 George Street, Romford, Essex.

According to the Commonwealth War Graves Commission website both John and William were killed during the war and we shall take a look at them shortly. The other one is shown on the Romford War Memorial as H. Pasfield, but when those details are searched on the same website, they draw a blank. According to their records there wasn't an H. Pasfield who was killed during the First World War. There was a Henry **Passfield** who was killed during the war but he had no known connection to Romford and his home address was in South Lambeth. There was a Henry James **Passfield** who served in the Royal Field Artillery during the war and who lived at number 24 Marks Road, Romford, Essex, but he survived, living the rest of his life in the town. He died in 1961 at the age 68.

On the First World War medal rolls index cards system, there is a Private (A/201597) Henry A.G. **Pasfield** who was a member of the Kings Royal Rifle Corps, but we could find no trace of him on either the Commonwealth War Graves Commission website, for those soldiers who had been killed during the war, or on the 1911 census so, regrettably, we have not been able to identify the H. **Pasfield** who is commemorated on the Romford War Memorial.

John **Pasfield** was a private (40365) serving in the 2nd Battalion, Northamptonshire Regiment, when he was killed on 31 July 1917. He was only 17 years of age, officially not old enough to have been serving at the front. He died during the Battle of the Somme and has no known grave. His name is commemorated on the Ypres (Menin Gate) War Memorial which is in the West Vlaanderen region of Belgium.

William **Pasfield** was a private (8760) serving in the 1st Battalion, Scots Guards, when he was killed a year after his younger brother, on 27 August 1918. He was 22 years of age and is buried at the Ligny-sur-Canche British cemetery in the Pas-de-Calais region of France.

The cemetery was begun at the end of August 1918 by the 19th and 43rd Casualty Clearing Stations, with burials there stopping only two

2

Freepost Plus RTKE-RGRJ-KTTX
Pen & Sword Books Ltd
47 Church Street
BARNSLEY
S70 2AS

DISCOVER MORE ABOUT MILITARY HISTORY

Pen & Sword Books have over 4000 books currently available, our imprints include; Aviation, Naval, Military, Archaeology, Transport, Frontline, Seaforth and the Battleground series, and we cover all periods of history on land, sea and air.

Keep up to date with our new releases by completing and returning the form below (no stamp required if posting in the UK).

Alternatively, if you have access to the internet, please complete your details online via our website at **www.pen-and-sword.co.uk.**

All those subscribing to our mailing list via our website will receive a free e-book, *Mosquito Missions* by Martin W Bowman. Please enter code number ACC1 when subscribing to receive your free e-book.

Mr/Mrs/Ms ....

Address...

....

Postcode................................ Email address...

Ligny-sur-Canche British Cemetery. (Wikipedia)

weeks later. William would have been one of the very first soldiers who was laid to rest in the quaint looking cemetery.

P. **Kronenberger**, a soldier with a Germanic sounding surname, was in fact half Belgian, his father, John Charles Kronenberger, having been born in Belgium in 1867.

Percy Charles **Kronenberger** was a rifleman (1400) in the 16th Battalion, London Regiment (Queens Westminster Rifles), when he was killed in action on 16 April 1915. He was born in Croydon, Surrey in 1894. He is buried at the Houplines Communal Cemetery Extension, which is located in the Nord region of France.

By the time the Commonwealth War Graves Commission began collating their records, Percy's parents, John and Rosa Kronenberger, had moved to 'Montrose', Brentwood Road, Romford, Essex, but the 1911 census shows the family were living at number 2 Briscoe Road, Hoddesdon in Hertfordshire.

The 16th Battalion, London Regiment (Queen's Westminster Rifles), were a territorial unit with its headquarters at 58 Buckingham Gate. They were part of the 4th London Brigade of the 2nd London Division.

Houplines Communal Cemetery Extension, Nord, France. (**Commonwealth War Graves Commission**)

Those wishing to join the Regiment had to pay twenty-five shillings to do so and the vast majority of its numbers were made up from clerical staff who worked in London offices.

The regiment was mobilized soon after the start of the war and moved to Hemel Hempstead in Hertfordshire, being billeted in Leverstock Green. They left for France via Southampton on 3 November 1914, landing at Le Havre later the same day to join the 18th Brigade, 6th Division. Their departure had been delayed due to German U-boat activity in the English Channel. The regiment was involved in fighting on the Western Front throughout most of the war and was finally demobilized on 18 May 1919.

Percy's name is not commemorated on the Croydon War Memorial, the town of his birth.

Jane Linsell has an interesting story. According to the 1901 census she was living at number 145, Albion Street, Romford, with her husband William who was 37 years old. They had five sons, William, Bertie, Ernest, Charles and Frederick. The latter two were both killed during the First World War. William and Ernest also served and survived, while Bertie, we could find no trace of him having served, although he was certainly old enough. Bertie died in 1969 at the age of 78.

William **Linsell** was in the 2nd Battalion, East Anglian Brigade, Royal Field Artillery. He enlisted on 8 May 1907 and was finally demobbed on 11 January 1919, having served in India and South Africa, as well as in the First World War.

Ernest was also in the Royal Field Artillery and he enlisted very early on in the war, on 31 August 1914.

By the end of the war Jane Linsell had moved, still in Romford, but to number 2, Wolsey Terrace, Rush Green. Her husband William had by this time passed away.

Frederick **Linsell** was a private (200339) in the 1st/4th Battalion, Essex Regiment, when he was killed on 26 March 1917 during the 1st Battle of Gaza when, as part of the Egyptian Expeditionary Force, he was involved in his battalion's attack on the Turkish held city of Gaza. He is buried in the Gaza War Cemetery in Palestine. He was the first of Jane's sons to be killed.

Charles **Linsell** was a private (34727) in the 1st Battalion, East

Surrey Regiment, when he was killed on 26 June 1918. He is buried at the Atal Wood Military Cemetery in Vieux-Berquin, Nord, France.

There is a third Linsell named on the Romford War Memorial, that of F.J. **Linsell**. We have found nothing to suggest he was an immediate family member, although he could have been a cousin. He was a rifleman (2752) in the 21st Battalion, London Regiment (East Surrey Rifles), when he was killed on 23 May 1915. He is buried at the Bethune town cemetery, Pas-de-Calais. He was 20 years of age at the time of his death. His parents, Joseph and Mary, lived at Brooklands Farm, North Street, Romford.

Stanley Richard James **Perry** was a proud scotsman born into a family where military tradition played a big part of everyday life. He was born at the Glencorse military barracks in Milton Bridge, Midlothian, home to the Royal Scots Regiment, where at the time his father, Peter Egbert Perry, was a colour sergeant.

In the 1911 census the family, with Peter Perry (retired from the military and now an army pensioner), were living at 57 Peabody Cottages, Herne Hill, London. Besides Peter and his wife Isabella, there was another son, Egbert, and two daughters, Cecilia and Petrina.

Stanley followed his father into the Royal Scots Regiment and became a sergeant in 'B' Company of the 2nd Battalion, although when he originally enlisted in the army it was as a private (1419) in the London Regiment. He died of wounds sustained at the Battle of the Somme on 21 July 1916. He is buried in the Dive Copse British Cemetery at Sailly-le-Sec, in the Somme region of France.

It isn't entirely obvious as to why Stanley is commemorated on the Romford War Memorial as his only connection to Romford would appear to be that when the Commonwealth War Graves Commission compiled their records, Stanley's mother had moved from Herne Hill to 38 Princes Road, Romford.

Stanley's brother Egbert also saw service during the First World War. He was attested on 11 December 1915 but wasn't mobilized for another nine months until 5 September 1916 when he became a signaller (164118) in 'C' Company Mountain Battery, Royal Field Artillery. He also served with the 15th Reserve Battery, the 6th Training Battery, 1205th Battery, and the 60th Reserve Battery.

He served in France for six months between January and July 1918 and on his return to England at the end of the war was hospitalized for five months between 20 December 1918 and 23 May 1919 suffering from bronchial pneumonia and influenza, believed to have been brought on by his constant exposure to the cold and rain while serving in France. Egbert survived both the war and his bout of flu and was demobilized on 9 July 1919.

A good example of the difficulties that can be connected with writing a book on military history is the case of the name of Taylor. The name Taylor appears on the Romford War Memorial four times in the shape of FC, FJ, L, and SRH Taylor.

S.R.H. stands for Stanley Ronald Horace **Taylor**, as recorded on the Commonwealth War Graves Commission website for private (14326) of the 6th Battalion, Royal Dublin Fusiliers who was killed on 9 August 1915 while fighting at Gallipoli. His name is commemorated on the Helles Memorial in Turkey.

The 1911 census shows the same 22-year-old Stanley living at Dene Villa, 83 Albert Road, Romford, with his parents, John and Sarah, his six brothers, and a sister. Jump back ten years to the 1901 census and they are living at 131 Marks Road, Romford and Stanley Ronald Horace Taylor is recorded as Stanley B. Taylor.

In the 1911 census, one of Stanley's brothers is shown as Frank G. Victor Taylor, but on the 1901 census he is shown as Frank J. Taylor. F.J. **Taylor** is one of the names recorded on the Romford War Memorial.

It is definitely the same family as in both the 1901 and 1911 censuses the details of the parents, John and Sarah A. Taylor are the same, down to their ages, location of where they were born and John's occupation of working on the railways.

Eric Alfred **Wright** had an affluent upbringing, his father, Alfred Wright, being a respected surgeon. Along with his parents and two sisters, Eric lived at 'The Lodge', South Street. The family employed four live-in servants to cook, clean and look after them.

Eric was an intelligent young man who, having decided to follow in his father's footsteps, went on to study medicine at Cambridge University. Having passed his exams and qualified to become a doctor, he set up his own practice in Romford.

On 4 April 1908 he became private 278 and joined the 14th

Battalion, County of London (London Scottish) Regiment, which were a Territorial Army unit.

The attestation (Army Form E. 502) which he had to complete contained fifteen questions. Question ten asked if the applicant currently belonged to any other military force. Eric answered that he did, the 7th Battalion, Middlesex Regiment. Question eleven asked if the applicant had previously belonged to another military force other than the one to which he currently belonged. Eric answered that he had previously belonged to the Cambridge University (4th Suffolk) Regiment. Question fourteen asked whether the applicant was willing to be attested for one, two, three or four years. Eric answered that he was willing to serve for one year, but at the end of that first year he signed on for a further year and continued to do so each year for the next five years. He was promoted to lance corporal in 1912, to full corporal on 29 August 1914 and to temporary lieutenant on 16 December 1914 when he was posted to the Royal Army Medical Corps.

He was killed on 21 June 1915 and is buried at the Alexandria (Chatby) Military and War Memorial Cemetery in Egypt.

Alexandria (Chatby) Military & War Memorial Cemetery. **(Commonwealth War Graves Commission)**

George and Frederick **Pead**, according to the 1911 census, lived at Low Shoe Lane, Collier Row, with their parents, George and Jeanett, four brothers and three sisters. They were the middle two of the six Pead brothers and the ones who would become victims of the war.

Henry, the youngest of the brothers, would have only been 12 years of age when the war started and still only 16 by the time it had finished, making him too young to have served in the war. Bertie, the next youngest of the brothers, we know lived until he was 81 years of age before he passed away in March 1979. The two oldest brothers, Charles and William, we can find no trace of them having ever served in the British Armed Forces during the First World War.

George **Pead** was a private (1026) in the 2nd Battalion, East Surrey Regiment when he was killed on 9 May 1915 during the Second Battle of Ypres. He was 20 years of age.

This battle saw the Germans release poison gas into the Allied lines just north of Ypres, the first time that either side had deployed such a tactic. The sheer violence of the German attack finally forced an allied withdrawal.

George's name is commemorated on the Ypres Menin Gate War Memorial which is for those who fell in the region during the war but whose bodies were never found and who have no known grave.

Frederick **Pead** was a sergeant (17033) in the 9th Battalion, Essex Regiment, when he was killed on 6 April 1918. He was 23 years of age. During April 1918, the allied 5th Army were driven back across the battlefields of the Somme by overwhelming German forces. It was during this fighting that Frederick was killed. His name is one of the 14,000 names of UK soldiers who are commemorated on the Pozières War Memorial. The names of some 300 South African soldiers are also commemorated on it. The memorial is for soldiers who are known to have fallen on the Somme between 21 March 1918 and 7 August 1918, and who have no known grave.

By the end of the war the remainder of the family had moved to number 2, White Hart Lane, Collier Row.

The surname of **Young** appears on the Romford War Memorial three times in the shape of CWC, RC, and HW **Young**, but they were not brothers. It's quite possible they were related in other ways but what, if any, connection there actually was between them, we have not been able to establish, except that they were all sons of Romford.

Charles William Cordeny **Young** was a private (531550) in the 1st/15th Battalion, London Regiment (Prince of Wales Civil Service Rifles), when he died on 2 September 1918 during the push by allied forces in Picardy and Artois. He was 20 years of age.

The family home was Mercury Nursery, Market Place. Mum and dad were William Henry and Emma Helen and there were two daughters and three other sons, none of whom were old enough to have fought in the war.

His name is commemorated on the Vis-en-Artois War Memorial which bears the names of 9,000 Commonwealth and South African soldiers who fell between 8 August 1918 and 11 November 1918 and who have no known grave.

Robert Charles **Young** was a private (11663) in the 9th Battalion, Devonshire Regiment, when he was killed on 6 September 1916. He was 21 years of age and his name is commemorated on the Thiepval War Memorial in Belgium.

His parents, Robert Charles and Betty, lived at number 9, St James Place, St Andrew's Road.

Herbert William **Young** was a lance corporal (3246) in the 12th Battalion, Royal Fusiliers, when he was killed on 15 April 1917 during the Arras Offensive, which took place between April and May of that year. He was 23 years of age and his name is commemorated on the Arras War Memorial.

Herbert's death made a widow of his beloved wife Alice. At the time of his death she was living at number 18, Lower Richmond Street.

Some of the names on war memorials all over the country were most certainly of a bygone era. Like the men behind them, most have been lost forever, but they are still old English names that should be cherished and remembered for evermore. Even some of the middle names were unusual to say the least. The next batch of names come into this category.

Walter Oggard **Westrop** was a private (L/9546) in the 4th Battalion, Royal Fusiliers, when he was killed on 24 August 1914 during the British Expeditionary Force's retreat from Mons. His name can be found on the La Ferté-sous-Jouarre War Memorial, which is situated in the Seine-et-Marne region of France. It commemorates 3,740 officers and men of the British Expeditionary Force who fell during the battles of Mons, Le Cateau, the Marne and the Aisne, between the end of August and the beginning of October 1914. It was unveiled on 4 November 1928 by Sir William Pulteney, who had commanded the III Corps of the British Expeditionary Force in 1914.

Walter's father Robert lived at number 114, George Street.

The name A. **Wopling** appears on the Romford War Memorial. A check on the Commonwealth War Graves Commission website shows a 49-year-old man who was a private (24315) in the 6th Battalion, Essex Regiment, who died on 12 March 1916 in Sevenoaks, Kent, suggesting that he was wounded while fighting abroad and brought home to a military hospital to have his wounds tended. It also shows that he was the husband of E. Wopling of 87 Quebec Road, Ilford, and that he is buried at Romford Cemetery. There are twenty-five other men who fell during the First World War who are buried there.

The 1911 census shows an Arthur Wopling, 44 years of age and married to Eliza Wopling. They had two daughters, Amy, who was 15, and Elsie, who was 9. They also had a son, Arthur, 12. They were living at number 49, Waterloo Road. Arthur senior was a labourer at one of the town's breweries.

Arthur Wopling junior was just 17 years of age in 1916 but, mysteriously, he also died in March of that year in Romford. We have found no trace of him having served in the military.

C.J. **Popplewell** is another of the names which appears on the Romford War Memorial. This was actually Charles Joseph Popplewell who was born in Romford in 1889.

The 1911 census shows that the Popplewell family lived at number 55, North Street. Besides Charles, who at 22 was the baby of the family, Mr and Mrs Robert James Popplewell had three daughters, Emily, 29, Charlotte, 25, and Victoria, 24.

Robert Popplewell was a master tailor by profession, while Charles was an assistant dentist when he decided to enlist in the army in his home town. He became a private (G/19890) and served in 2nd Battalion, Royal Sussex Regiment. He died of his wounds on 15 November 1917 while serving on the Western Front and is buried at the Vlamertinghe New Military Cemetery in the West-Vlaanderen

Vlamertinghe New Military Cemetery. **(Commonwealth War Graves Commission)**

region of Belgium. Most of the 1,813 Commonwealth soldiers who are buried there were killed between July and December 1917.

A.J. **Pharoah**, or Alfred James **Pharoah** to be precise, was the husband of Maud who lived at number 84, Willow Street.

During the First World War he was a private (270219) in the 1st Battalion, Bedfordshire Regiment, although initially he joined the Royal West Kent Regiment with whom he served from his enlistment on 26 February 1916 until his transfer to the Bedfordshire Regiment on 1 April 1918. Five months later, at the age of 37, he was dead, killed on 23 August 1918.

He is buried in the Adanac Military Cemetery at Miraumont, Somme, France. The cemetery acquired its name because many of those buried there were brought in from the Canadian battlefields in and around Courcelette and Miraumont. The name is 'Canada' spelt backwards.

Adanac Military Cemetery, Miraumont. **(Commonwealth War Graves Commission)**

Out of the 3,186 Commonwealth soldiers who are buried in the cemetery, a staggering 1,708 of them are unidentified.

A. **Ellingworth** was Arthur William Ellingworth who lived at Dagnam Park Lodge with his wife Minnie whom he had married at Romford Parish Church on 26 October 1908. They had a son, Eric Arthur William. Arthur's parents, Charles and Elizabeth, also lived in Romford, in the High Street.

Arthur was a gunner (283034) in the Royal Garrison Artillery when he died aged 43 on 5 May 1918. He is buried in St Thomas's Churchyard, Noak Hill. Before the war he had been a reservist.

He first enlisted on a seven-year short service contract in the army on 27 August 1896 when he joined the Royal Artillery as a gunner (16289). He was a month short of his twenty-first birthday and had previously been a cellarman working in a local pub. After fulfilling his commitment to serve in the Royal Artillery, he was transferred to the Army Reserve on 21 March 1904, before being finally discharged on 1 September 1908 having served for four years 164 days. His service saw him stationed in Gibraltar for nearly five years between 17 November 1897 and 11 October 1902. From there he was posted to Malta, arriving there on 12 October 1902. It would be nearly a year and a half before he returned home to England, leaving Malta on 19 March 1904, meaning he had served abroad continuously for nearly six and a half years.

He was reattested on 10 December 1915 before being mobilized three months later on 7 March 1916, only lasting eighteen months before being discharged from the army on 11 September 1917, having been found to be no longer physically fit enough for war service. He died eight months later on 5 May 1918 having never been posted abroad during the hostilities, quite possibly because of a combination of his age and the previous experiences he had evidently had. His wife

*St Thomas's Churchyard,
Noak Hill.*
**(Commonwealth War
Graves Commission)**

Minnie was awarded a pension of twenty-one shillings and eight pence a week for her and their young child.

R. **Crudgington** was a rifleman (45485) in the 11th Battalion, Rifle Brigade (The Prince Consort's Own), when he was killed on 13 June 1918, although he originally enlisted in the 1st/13th Battalion, London Regiment, as a private (493146). He had also served as a private (5864) with the Middlesex Regiment during the war. It was not unusual for men to find themselves part of different battalions or even regiments because of the heavy losses which were sustained by some units.

He is buried in the Sucrerie Cemetery in Ablain-Saint-Nazaire in the Pas-de-Calais region of France.

Richard Crudgington was awarded both the Victory Medal and the British War Medal for his services to his country during the First World War.

Along with his parents, John and Sarah, and his three elder brothers, Charles, Harry and James, Richard lived at number 82, High Street. Before the war Richard was a local fishmonger.

R.G. Alabaster was in fact Roger George **Alabaster**, a rifleman (303973) in the 1st/15th Battalion, London Regiment (London Rifles). He was killed on 16 August 1917 aged 25. His name is commemorated on the Ypres (Menin Gate) War Memorial.

Roger's parents, George and Mary Ellen Ann, lived at 257 Crown Road after the war, but before it they had lived at number 8 Alpine Terrace, Pretoria Road, along with their three daughters and their three other sons, none of whom were anywhere near old enough to have served in the army during the First World War.

Thomas and Martha Wraight lived at 'Inglebrae', Erroll Road, with their three sons, Bernard, born in 1884, Oswald, born in 1892, and Wilfred, born in 1896. They also had two daughters, Lilian, who like her brother Bernard was born in 1884, and Muriel, born in 1890.

All three sons served their king and country during the First World War. Bernard was a private (9780) in the Honourable Artillery Company. Oswald was a corporal (531910) in the 15th Battalion, London Regiment (Prince of Wales's Own Civil Service Rifles), and Wilfred was a lance corporal in the 4th Battalion, Essex Regiment, which was a Territorial unit which, when first mobilized after the outbreak of the war, was billeted at nearby Brentwood Grammar school.

Before the war Bernard had been a draper, the profession to which he returned after the fighting finished. He went on to live to the ripe old age of 89 before passing away in 1973, still living in his beloved Romford.

Neither Oswald nor Wilfred were so fortunate. Wilfred was the first to be killed, on 25 November 1917 while his battalion was serving as part of the Egyptian Expeditionary Force who were fighting their way to Jerusalem. He was 22 years of age. By 21 November 1917 the Force had advanced to within five kilometres west of the city, which had been deliberately spared an artillery bombardment because of concerns over the damage to the historic city. This resulted in fierce and bloody fighting on the ground which continued until the evening of 8 December 1917 when the 53rd division in the south and the 60th and 74th Divisions in the west had captured all of the city's prepared defences. It was during this fighting that Wilfred was killed.

The Turkish forces finally left Jerusalem overnight on 8 December and the following morning the Mayor of Jerusalem handed the Turkish governors a letter of surrender to the Allied commanders. On 11 December 1917 General Allenby, along with his French and Italian counterparts, formally entered the sacred city. Although Turkish forces made subsequently attempts to retake the city, it remained in Allied hands until the end of the war.

Oswald was killed nine months later on 30 August 1918. He is buried in the Daours Communal Cemetery Extension which is located ten kilometres east of Amiens. It was unveiled on 7 May 1927 by the now Lord Allenby and Sir James Parr. The cemetery closed only a matter of days after Oswald was buried there.

Mr and Mrs Wraight had to deal with great sadness: the death of two of their sons. Thankfully they were also able to experience the joy of the return home of Bernard.

The 1911 census shows that Frederick and Eleanor Warman lived at number 40 Hamilton Road, Heath Park, along with their two teenage sons, George, who was 16, and Percy, 13.

Frederick worked as a machine attendant, George was a labourer, and Percy was an apprentice grocer, while Eleanor looked after the family home, cleaning and cooking for the three men in her life.

George was a private (200254) in the 4th Battalion, Essex Regiment, when he was killed on 27 March 1917 aged 22. At the time of his death the battalion was part of the Egyptian Expeditionary Force that were fighting their way towards Jerusalem. George's name is commemorated on the Jerusalem War Memorial.

Percy was a lance corporal (27040) in the 2nd Battalion, Duke of Edinburgh's (Wiltshire Regiment), although when he initially enlisted in the army it had been as a private in his local Essex Regiment, the same as his brother George.

He was killed in action during intense fighting on 2 June 1917. At the time of his death he was 19 years of age. He is buried at the Ramparts Cemetery, Lille Gate, which is in the West-Vlaanderen region of Belgium.

Headstone of Lance Corporal Percy A. Warman.

Not only did Mr and Mrs Warman have to contend with the death of their elder son George, but while still grieving their loss, four months later they had to deal with the loss of their younger son, Percy. The pain and suffering which they must have experienced with the loss of both of their sons, who were also their only children, can only be guessed at, and to have lost them so close together undoubtedly added to their anguish.

Ramparts Cemetery, Lille Gate. (Commonwealth War Graves Commission)

Thomas and Lucinda Horsnail had three children, Linda, who at 22 years of age was their eldest, Francis Walter, who was 18, and Johnson Alfred John, who was only 12 at the time of the 1911 census. At that time the family are shown as living at Eastbrook End Cottages, Dagenham, but by the end of the war the family have moved to Rathbone Villa, Wolseley Road, Rush Green, Romford.

Johnson Alfred John Horsnail was a private (35977) in the 8th Battalion, Gloucestershire Regiment, when he was killed on 15 April 1918 aged 19. His name is commemorated on the Tyne Cot War Memorial which is situated in the West-Vlaanderen region of Belgium.

Before the war, Francis Walter Horsnail was a mechanical engineer, single, and at 21 years of age when the war broke out was a prime candidate to be called up. We have found no record of Francis having served in any of His Majesty's armed services. Sadly for his parents though, Francis died a month before Johnson was killed, while serving on the Western Front. It can only be assumed that he was one of the victims of the flu pandemic which took place between January 1918 and December 1920 which, unlike previous outbreaks, predominantly killed previously healthy young adults.

There are nearly 35,000 officers and men from the Commonwealth nations who fell during the First World War named on the Tyne Cot War Memorial and who have no known grave, an absolutely staggering number. There are also nearly 12,000 Commonwealth servicemen buried in Tyne Cot's Cemetery. Just over 8,000 of these men have no known identity.

The Tyne Cot War Memorial was unveiled by Sir Gilbert Dyett on 20 June 1927.

CHAPTER 3

Romford's Military Connections

Entrance to Hare Hall Army Camp. (**Permission Brian Evans,** *A Century of Romford*)

Romford and its neighbouring towns and villages had numerous military connections during the First World War.

One was the army camp at Hare Hall, Upper Brentwood Road, near to Gidea Park Railway Station. The camp had two famous occupants during the First World War in the form of the 24th Battalion, Royal Fusiliers, better known as the 2nd Sportsman's Battalion, and later the 2nd Battalion, Artists Rifles, Officer Training Corps. Once trained and commissioned as officers, the men went on to serve with numerous other Regiments throughout the British army.

The 2/28th (County of London) Battalion (Artists Rifles) were formed right at the beginning of the war, in August 1914, in London. They later moved to Richmond Park and in July 1915 they moved on to High Beech in Epping Forest.

Officers listening to the camp's band.
(Permission Brian Evans, *A Century of Romford*)

Ors Communal Cemetery.
(Commonwealth War Graves
Commission)

In November 1915 the 1/28th Battalion, who were in France at the time, was recognized as an officers' training corps and absorbed the 2/28th Battalion. By March1916 it had moved to Hare Hall at Romford where it then became Number 15 Officer Cadet Battalion, where it remained for the remainder of the war.

War poets Edward Thomas and Wilfred Owen both trained at Hare Hall. The other thing which they sadly had in common was that neither of them survived the war. Thomas was killed in 1917 and Owen was killed just a week before the end of the war, on 4 November 1918.

Wilfred Edward Salter had enlisted in the Artists Rifles in October 1915 and was commissioned as a lieutenant into the 5th Battalion, Manchester Regiment, in June 1916. He was a holder of the Military Cross. He is buried at the Ors Communal Cemetery in the Nord region of France where there are approximately sixty graves of servicemen who fell during the First World War. The village of Ors sits between the town of Landrecies and Le Cateau and has two cemeteries, one is the Communal Cemetery, and the other is the British cemetery.

Grey Towers Camp, Hornchurch

The 1st Sportsman's Battalion, 23rd Battalion Royal Fusiliers, under the command of Colonel Viscount Maitland, was billeted at barracks at Grey Towers Camp, about two miles away from Hare Hall. Grey Towers Park had been placed at the disposal of the battalion by the family of its owner, the late Colonel Holmes.

Most battalions during the First World War were raised by well-

Grey Towers Camp, Hornchurch.

known individuals of the day, often members of the Royal Family. The Sportsman's Battalion wasn't raised by anybody of such high social standing, but by Mrs Cunliffe-Owen, the daughter of the late Sir P. Cunliffe-Owen.

The 1st Sportsman's Battalion, 23rd Battalion, Royal Fusiliers (City of London Regiment), were almost the equivalent of the SAS of their day. Fitness levels to be accepted into the battalion were of a much higher standard than other regiments of the British army. Recruits were accepted up to 45 years of age.

The 2nd Sportsman's Battalion, 24th Battalion, Royal Fusiliers (City of London Regiment), numbering well over 1,000 men and looking resplendent in their uniforms, presented a fine appearance as they arrived at the Hare Hall camp for the first time on Wednesday, 17 March 1915. Their commanding officer was Colonel A. de B.V. Paget who had previously served for twenty-eight years in the Durham Light Infantry including during the Tirah campaign in India of 1897-98. He also held the prestigious title of His Majesty's Honourable Corps of Gentleman-at-Arms.

At the time, the Hare Hall camp was seen as the most up-to-date and prestigious field barracks that had ever been erected anywhere in England. Each of the fifty accommodation huts in the barracks held thirty men. These were laid out in a street formation. The huts were timber framed which were then covered in galvanized iron sheeting. The internal walls were boarded so as to provide better insulation. The roofs were painted in brick red with the outer walls either dark green or dark brown, and the floors were made of wooden boards. Each of the huts had electricity, in a time when candles were still the main order of the day. There was a guardroom, stores, cookhouse, drying rooms, canteen and a toilet block (which at the time was referred to as the ablutions shed). There were twenty-four shower baths with hot and cold running water for use by the men, and the entire camp was lit by electricity which was generated by a dynamo. There was a boot-makers' hut, one that was the camp's post office, another was the tailor's, and one was the barber's, and a sergeants' mess. The ovens in the cookhouse were designed to have a capacity to cook 550 dinners at a time.

In the main building the bedrooms had been neatly and simply furnished to accommodate thirty-six officers, while the subalterns slept four to a room. The battalion's colonel had one of the smallest rooms, which looked out over the camp and was no more resplendent than any of those occupied by his junior officers.

The camp also boasted its own hospital, with twenty-four beds, the Royal Army Medical Corps from Colchester supplying a sergeant and five men to form the nursing staff. There was also a dispensary.

In 1915 such facilities really were luxuries. Only the very rich would have been able to afford equivalent living standards. Even the facilities at the Grey Towers camp at Hornchurch, where the 1st Sportsman's Battalion were stationed, hadn't been as good.

For several weeks before they arrived on 4 November 1914, there had been hundreds of workmen in Grey Towers Park erecting the accommodation huts and the other buildings which were required for the smooth running of the new camp.

By the end of the war the Battalion had lost a total of 944 officers and men who had either been killed in action, died of their wounds, were missing in action or who had died from sickness while on active service. Another 2,297 officers and men were wounded.

In the book *Hornchurch during the Great War*, written by Charles Thomas Perfect and first published in 1921, there is a list of some of the men of the 1st Sportsman's Battalion who first graced the camp with their presence. These names had been gleaned from the *Sportsman Gazette*, which was a weekly magazine published by the Sportsman's Battalion. We have replicated their names below but added in whether they fell in the war or survived it.

Private (115) William **Albany** was a world champion sculler. He went on to become a corporal in the 23rd Battalion, Royal Fusiliers, and was awarded a Military Medal for his bravery. He was killed in action on 2 August 1916 aged 30 and is buried in the Corbie Communal Cemetery Extension, Somme, France, about fifteen kilometres east of the city of Amiens. William's wife lived at number 16, Rotherwood Road, Putney, London.

Private William E. **Bates** was a county cricketer who represented Yorkshire. Although he began the war in the Royal Fusiliers as lance sergeant (919) he finished the war as a sapper (156550) in the Royal Engineers. He was awarded the 1915 Star, along with the Victory Medal and the British War Medal.

Private Brian Danvers **Butler**, the son of the 6th Earl of Lanesborough, Captain John Vansittart Danvers Butler, was something of an all-round sportsman, particularly golf and cricket. At the outbreak of the war, when he enlisted in the army, he was already 38 years of age. Sadly he did not survive the war; he was killed on 18 August 1916 during the Battle of the Somme, by which time he had reached the rank of 2nd lieutenant and had transferred to the Kings Royal Rifle Corps, more than likely when he was commissioned. At the time of his death he was serving with the 7th Battalion of the regiment.

His name is commemorated on the Thiepval War Memorial for those who have no known grave. His brother, Francis Almeric Butler, who was a captain in the Hampshire Yeomanry, survived the war. The British Army First World War medal rolls index cards show that Francis was ineligible for the British War Medal, the Victory Medal and the 1915 Star, but there is no explanation as to why this is so.

Lieutenant Norman Alexander Lindsay **Cockell** was not only regarded as the best all-round sportsman in the battalion but also the best shot. Norman served in France but didn't stay with the Sportsman's Battalion. He transferred to the 20th Battalion and then some time after that moved on to the 13th Battalion, Bedfordshire Regiment, the last transfer being on promotion to captain, the rank at which he finished the war.

Private Colin Campbell Rae **Brown** was an unusual character in so far as he wasn't a renowned sportsman but a well-known author of his day who had written many crime thriller novels. Seeing as he had books published in 1920, 1922, 1923, 1924 and 1930, it would be a safe bet to assume with some degree of certainty that he survived the war.

Private L. **Carter** was a well-known engineer. The British Army First World War medal rolls index cards show that there was an L. Carter who had originally been a member of the Royal Fusiliers (2073) but doesn't clarify which battalion he had served with, before transferring to the Royal Flying Corps (166112).

Sergeant Philip Howard **Cooper** had been an Anglican clergyman before the war. While serving with the Sportsman's Battalion he had been promoted to the rank of lieutenant before becoming a captain and transferring to the Machine Gun Corps. He was awarded the British War medal, the Victory medal and the 1915 Star. He survived, and after the war was living at Burley, near Brockenhurst in Hampshire.

Private James Herbert **Curle** was a mining engineer and an author. He survived the war and died in 1942 when 72 years of age. In 1921 he had a book published entitled *This World of Ours*. In 1926 he published another, *Today and Tomorrow the Testing Period of the White Race*, and in 1927 he published *The Shadow Show*. A book he had published in 1899 had the exceptionally long title of *The Gold Mines of the World, containing concise and practical advice for investors gathered from a personal inspection of the mines of the Transvaal, India, West Australia, Queensland, New Zealand, British Columbia and Australia*. Quite possibly the longest title of a book ever.

Sergeant Major **Cumming** was a champion race walker. When searching the Commonwealth War Graves Commission website for the surname Cumming, 162 names are displayed, but none of them were a sergeant major serving with the Royal Fusiliers. That it is not to say of course that he had not been promoted in rank or had transferred to another regiment prior to the end of the war. We were unable to find a matching service record for anybody who had served with the Royal Fusiliers.

Lance Corporal (633) Claude Frederick **Canton** had previously been a big game hunter as well as having served in the Matabele Mounted Police between 1896 and 1898. When he enlisted in the army in London on 14 October 1914, at the age of 36, his occupation was shown as sugar planter, which is partially confirmed by the fact that he does not appear on either the 1901 or the 1911 English census.

After a year of training at different locations around Britain, he arrived in France on 16 November 1915. He survived the war, at the end of which he was a private (602557) in the 837 Company, Labour Corps. When he was discharged, on 5 March 1919, Claude was 41 years of age. He was awarded the 1915 Star, the British War Medal and the Victory Medal. Although living at Minters Farm in Capel Saint Mary, near Ipswich in Suffolk, he actually died at number 43, Priory Road in Hampstead in March 1937 at the relatively young age of 59. In his will he left £495 15 shillings and 9 pence (which translates as £30,000 today).

Lance Corporal (1343) George **de Lara** was a celebrated actor at the time of his enlistment on 5 January 1915, when he was already 43 years of age. He was posted to 'B' Company, 23rd Battalion, Royal Fusiliers. Fifteen months later, on 3 April 1916, his war was over after he was discharged under paragraph 392 of the Kings Regulations for being no longer physically fit for war. He spent the first ten months of his service in England; he then served with the British Expeditionary Force in France from 16 November 1915 to 7 January 1916 before returning home and being admitted to Wharncliffe War Hospital in Sheffield. He was there until 22 February 1916, and on his release was given a nine-day furlough. His home address was shown as being at 12 Brook Street, Kensington, London. There was no explanation as to what ailment or injury had resulted in his admission to hospital, but there was the following entry on his paperwork: 'Fit for light duty and likely to be fit for service overseas within three months.' Yet, as we know, just five weeks later rather than returning to overseas service he had returned to civvy street. In 1920 he was awarded the 1914-15 Star, the British War Medal and the Victory Medal, by which time he was now living at number 28 Cromwell Road, East Finchley, London N2.

Private Albert Edward **Dunn** had previously been the Mayor of Exeter as well as the MP for Camborne in Cornwall before enlisting in the army.

Albert was born on 13 February 1864, so by the time the First World War had begun he was already 50 years of age. As the upper age for being accepted in to the Sportsman's Battalion

Albert Edward Dunn
(Circa 1906).
(Wikipedia)

was 45, how he managed to get in isn't exactly clear. He was a member of the Liberal Party when he first stood for election to Parliament in the general election of 1892 at the very young age, for a politician, of 28. He was unsuccessful in his attempts at winning the seat of Exeter from the Conservatives. It would be another fourteen years, in 1906, before he would try again. This time he was successful and he became the MP for Camborne in Cornwall. He was re-elected in the General Election of January and February of 1910 which resulted in a hung parliament where power was shared between the Conservatives and the Liberals. The alliance didn't last long and a second General Election took place in December of the same year. Albert decided not to contest the seat again and stood down. Albert survived the war and died on 2 May 1937 aged 71.

Private F. **Darley-Crozier** was the son of Major General H. Darley-Crozier and a topical planter. There was no sign of his name on the Commonwealth War Graves Commission website for those recorded as having been killed during the First World War, nor could I find a service record for him. There was no trace of him on the 1911 census.

Private A.B. **Day** was a world champion runner. We could find nothing further about Private Day.

Private Charlie **Dillon** was a well-known comedian before the war.

Corporal (SPTS/1431) Jeremiah 'Jerry' **Delaney** was a lightweight boxing champion of England prior to enlisting in the army. He was killed on 27 July 1916 during the Battle of the Somme, one of eighty members of the battalion who met their death that fateful day. His name is commemorated on the Thiepval War Memorial along with those of 72,000 other officers and men who died during the Battle of the Somme and who have no known grave.

Private J.D. **Driver** was a member of the London Stock Exchange, and a well-known tennis player and umpire.

Private (395) Cyril Charles **Freer** was a journalist with the *Daily Mail* newspaper before he enlisted in the army at the relatively old age for a soldier of 40. He later became 2nd editor of the *Sportsman's Gazette*. He didn't stay with the Sportsman's Battalion; he was commissioned as a lieutenant and transferred to the Middlesex Regiment. He survived the war and returned to live in London at 68 & 69 Avenue Chambers, Vernon Place, Southampton Row. A Yorkshire man by birth, he died in Middlesex in March 1956 aged 82.

Private (GS/73190) Charles Edward **Gaskell** was one of the best all-round sportsmen in the north of England and was known as the 'Baby' of Hut 25, 'Unity Hall'. He lived at number 33, High Street, Portwood, Stockport, Cheshire, along with his mother Emily Jane. His father James had already passed away by the time of the 1911 census. He had a brother James who was three years older than him. Their 73-year-old grandfather, also called James, lived with them as well. He survived the war and reached the rank of warrant officer 2nd class, staying with the Royal Fusiliers throughout the war.

His brother James was old enough to have served during the war, but we have not been able to identify him with any degree of certainty. There are only two service records available for individuals named James Gaskell who served in the First World War, but neither of them is shown as having been born in Stockport, Cheshire as James was. On the Commonwealth War Graves Commission website there are three individuals by the name of James Gaskell. Two of them were killed in 1918. One of them was 31 years of age while the other was 26. The James Gaskell I am looking for would have only been 23 years of age in 1918. The entry for the third person of the same name does not include enough information to be able to definitely identify him as Charles's brother.

Corporal T.W. **Greenstreet** was a lecturer in English History before he enlisted in the army. The Commonwealth War Graves Commission website, British army service records, and the British army pension records show various numbers of men with the name of Greenstreet who served in the First World War but none have the initials TW or are shown as serving with the Royal Fusiliers. The British army medal rolls index for the First World War shows that sixty-six officers and men with the surname Greenstreet were awarded service medals. One of them does have the initials TW, Thomas William Greenstreet, but he did not serve with the Sportsman's Battalion, Royal Fusiliers. He served as a 2nd lieutenant with the Northern Regiment, attached to the Royal Inniskilling Fusiliers before returning to his parent regiment as a lieutenant with the 3rd Battalion. Along with the British War and Victory medals, he was awarded the Military Cross. Having said all of that we cannot conclusively prove this is the same T.W. Greenstreet who served with the Sportsman's Battalion.

Colonel Alfred St Hill **Gibbons** was 2nd in command of the

Sportsman's Battalion at Hornchurch. He is reported, in the book *Hornchurch during the Great War* by Charles Thomas Perfect, to have discovered the source of the Zambezi River and was a well-known big game hunter. He did not survive the war, being killed in France. When he was a major, Gibbons led two expeditions to the upper basin and central course of the Zambezi. The first of these took place between 1895 and 1896 and then again two years later between 1898 and 1900. The first European to come across the Zambezi River was the Portuguese explorer Vasco da Gama in January 1498. In 1884, Frederick Stanley Arnot, a Plymouth Brethren missionary, who was accompanied by Antonio da Silva Porto, a Portuguese army officer, identified the source of the Zambezi. Where Charles Thomas Perfect obtained the information for his book back in 1921, about Colonel Gibbons having discovered the source of the Zambezi River, is therefore somewhat unclear. At the time of his death, on 15 July 1916, two weeks in to the Battle of the Somme, Gibbons held the rank of temporary lieutenant colonel and commanded the 13th Battalion, Kings (Liverpool) Regiment. He had previously been mentioned in despatches for his bravery and leadership.

Private Ernest G. **Hayes** played cricket for Surrey.

Private (352) J.W. **Hitch** played cricket for Surrey and was a famous fast bowler. He enlisted in the army early on in the war, on 6 October 1914, but less than six months later, on 1 April 1915, his war was over before it had even started. It had been decided by his instructors and senior officers that he was not likely to become an efficient soldier and that within three months of enlisting he was considered unfit for service. This was in line with the Kings Regulation 392 (iii c). It can only be assumed that it had nothing to do with his level of fitness, as he had previously been a fast bowler for Surrey, but there was no explanation why he was deemed to be unfit. Maybe it was a long-standing injury that he had either hidden from the authorities or that he simply didn't know about.

Private Elias Henry **Hendren**, who was better known by his nickname of 'Patsy', played for Middlesex County Cricket Club and England as well as previously having played football for Coventry City and Manchester City.

Elias Henry Hendren.
(Wikipedia)

In the 1911 census he shows as being a boarder with a Mr and Mrs Lawrence of number 2 Gresham Street, Coventry, and his occupation is shown as being that of a professional cricketer. He survived the war and returned to being a professional cricketer playing in his first England test match in the December 1920 series against Australia in Sydney. He would play another fifty test matches for England, the last of which was against the West Indies in Kingston, Jamaica, in March 1935 when he was 46 years of age. His highest test score was 205 not out. He scored 7 centuries and 21 half-centuries and ended up with a very creditable test batting average of 47.63. He also played 833 first class matches for Middlesex, where his highest score was 301 not out and his batting average was 50.80. His 170 first class centuries still places him as one of the best batsmen of all time. He also hit 272 half-centuries while playing for Middlesex. Excluding the war years, his first class cricket career lasted for thirty years, from 1907 to 1937. He died at the Whittington Hospital in Tooting Bec on 4 October 1962 aged 73. His home address was shown as 310 Scot Ellis Gardens, Grove End Road, London NW8.

Lance Corporal (SPTS/348) James Michael **Hendren** had played cricket for Durham and Middlesex before the war. He was killed nearly a month in to the Battle of the Somme on 27 July 1916. His has no known grave and his name is on the Thiepval War Memorial.

Private (1467) Jack **Harrison** was a well-known boxer of the day, a winner of a Lonsdale belt at middleweight in 1912. He became the British middleweight boxing champion on 20 May 1912, but never defended his title. He had previously served in the Grenadier Guards between 1907 and 1910. Jack Harrison enlisted in to the 23rd Service Battalion, Royal Fusiliers, on 28 January 1915 at Hornchurch. He was 26 years of age. On his attestation form, question number five asks, 'What is your trade or calling?' Jack's reply was 'Pugilist,' the poshest way it is possible to say 'Boxer'! He married Mary Jane Fathers, a widow, on 16 September 1918 in Wellingborough. She had a son from her previous marriage, Fredrick William Fathers, who was born in 1909 in Nuneaton. The likelihood was that her husband had been killed in the war. Jack served with the Sportsman's Battalion until 16 May 1917, then in the space of four months he had been transferred to the 5th Battalion, Royal Fusiliers, then the 13th, and the 24th. The reason for these transfers would appear to be because he had fractured his collar bone while working with the 254th Tunnelling Company, Royal Engineers. He had arrived in France on 23 August 1917 with his battalion and three weeks later, on 13 September 1917, he transferred to the 106th Company, Labour Corps, with whom he was promoted to the rank of corporal (385554), on 6 April 1918. On 14 February 1919, Jack sailed from Dieppe on route to England with orders to report to the Discharge Centre at Purfleet in Essex. Like most who had served during the Great War, Jack had to wait nearly three years before he received his wartime medals.

Private William J. **Harvey** was the first editor of the battalion's *Sportsman's Gazette* magazine. He is also an excellent example of just how difficult it can be for somebody to research individuals from the First World War and know with any degree of certainty that they have found the individual for whom they are looking. On the Commonwealth War Graves Commission website there is a William J. Harvey who lived in Plaistow in the East End of London. He was a private (G/4420) in the 2nd Battalion and at the time of his death on 28 February 1917 he was 42 years of age. What has to be remembered is that these are the regiments and battalions that the soldier was in at the time of his death, which is not necessarily the same as the ones he was in when he first enlisted. The point is that there is no way of knowing if this is the same person who I am looking for with any degree of certainty.

By way of further explanation about the difficulties of researching soldiers from the First World War, consider if you will the difficulties connected with this next example. Searching William J. Harvey in the British Army First World War medal rolls index throws up forty-four men with that exact same name. They in turn belong to thirty-three different regiments and only one of these started out with the Royal Fusiliers, but even he transferred to another regiment (the Hampshire) during the war, so depending on the record being checked, it might only show William J. Harvey, Hampshire Regiment and not the Royal Fusiliers.

Captain Stanley **Holmes** was the son of the late lieutenant colonel Henry Homes of Grey Towers. The 1901 census shows Stanley, who was 33 at the time, living at Grey Towers with his parents, Henry and

Emilie, along with five servants to look after them. By the time of the 1911 census, Stanley has moved out and his father Henry is 82 years of age. He had five brothers and sisters and his parents had been married for forty-seven years, meaning that his mother was only 18 years of age on her wedding day while Henry would have been 35.

Private Douglas **Henderson** was like lots of young men of the time, adventurous, driven, passionate and somebody who wanted excitement in his life. This mindset was the main reason why he was an explorer. Before the war he had spent six years travelling the world. When he decided to enlist in the army, the allure and the stature of the Sportsman's Battalion would have been just the type of challenge for which he would have been looking. The main difficulty with properly identifying the Douglas Henderson mentioned in Charles Perfect's book is that there were three men with that name who served with the Royal Fusiliers and at least two of them served with the 23rd Battalion. Private 1077 Douglas Henderson was with the 23rd Battalion. He was discharged from the army on 12 September 1917 because he was deemed to be no longer fit for war service. Private 42 Douglas Henderson originally served with the Royal Fusiliers before transferring to the Labour Corps. He survived the rigours of the war and was demobbed on 10 February 1919. Private GS/93389 Douglas Henderson had previously served as a Private (73726) in the Durham Light Infantry, of the city of his birth. He died of his wounds on 1 October 1918 and is buried in the Grevillers British Cemetery in the Pas-de-Calais. There are 2,016 Commonwealth servicemen, 189 of which are unidentified, who fell during the First World War who are either buried or commemorated in the cemetery.

Will the real Douglas Henderson please stand up? This is as close as we can get to finding the identity of the man for whom we are looking.

Private Richard **Kendall**, service number Spts/982, was an actor by profession. He landed in France on 16 November 1915. For his wartime service he was awarded the 1915 Star, the British War Medal and the Victory Medal.

Private J.M. **Kendall** was an antiquary, a fellow of the Society of Archaeologists, and a writer.

Lance Corporal Edward **Leith** was a songwriter and stage manager.

Grevillers British Cemetery. (**Commonwealth War Graves Commission**)

Sergeant R.T. **Noyes** was one of the most popular men in the Battalion. He was an all-round sportsman, a ranconteur affectionately known as 'Canada', and was part of the relief expedition to Gordon of Khartoum.

Private A. **Sandrum** had played cricket for Surrey before the outbreak of the war.

Lieutenant (SPTS/883) Robert de Vere **Stacpoole** had been 43 years of age when he enlisted in the 23rd Battalion, Royal Fusiliers. He had previously served in the British army in the 6th Dragoon Guards but that had been some years earlier and he had been discharged back in 1902. The second time round, he enlisted two months into the war on 6 October 1914. He had only been with the Sportsman's Battalion for about seven weeks when he was discharged from the Royal Fusiliers to take up his commission as an officer on 26 November 1914. Sometime during the war, he transferred from the Royal Fusiliers to the West African Free Force, where he was also a lieutenant. After the war he went to live in Scarborough.

Private Denis **Turner** was an author and a contributor to *Punch* and *Vanity Fair*.

Private (SPTS/634) Alfred Henry **Toogood** was a professional golfer who represented England against Scotland in 1904, 1905, 1906 and 1907 before he enlisted in the army. He was born on 1 May 1872 in St Helens on the Isle of Wight. Alfred was naturally gifted in the finer points of the sport of golf and, with the added desire to be as good as he could possibly be, he took part in the British Open Championship in 1894, at the age of 22. That year it was played at the Royal St George golf course at Sandwich in Kent, which was the first time in its thirty-four year existence that it had been held outside Scotland. Out of ninety-four competitors he finished a creditable fourth place, which won him the princely sum of £7. This would ultimately prove to have been his best performance of the four appearances he would make in the British Championship in subsequent years. Alfred survived the war and died in 1921.

Private E.S. **Vincer** was a marine engineer and had been a bullfighter in Cartagena, Spain in 1912. When searching for the army service record of E.S. Vincer I came across one for a Frederick George **Vincer**, who was only 19 when he enlisted in the East Lancashire Regiment. He too was from Cartagena in Spain, most likely a younger brother. We also found an Edward Seccombe **Vincer**, but there was no record of him having ever been in the 23rd Battalion, Royal Fusiliers. He was, however, a lieutenant in the 4th Battalion, Royal Dublin Fusiliers, the Royal Flying Corps and the Royal Air Force, which shows he was alive in 1918, as the Royal Air Force didn't come into existence until 1 April 1918. On the balance of probabilities, they are one and the same person, but the ambiguity over there being no mention of the 23rd Battalion, Royal Fusiliers, leaves an element of uncertainty.

Corporal Alfred Burden **Wharton** was a comedian and a well-known London entertainer.

Private J.J. **Williams** (Julian Brandon) was a well-known conjuror, entertainer, journalist and lecturer on psychology.

Private (823) Frank **Winchcombe**, like a lot of his colleagues, was an all-round sportsman, being able to turn his hand to most sports to a more than useful degree.

Private D.R. **Warner** had the massive claim to fame that he was the cousin of General Sir Douglas Haig. Whether or not the family connection was of any use to him has not been recorded. It might not have even been a widely-known fact amongst his immediate peers.

The Honourable Bernard Elliot **Yorke** was a well-known sportsman and game hunter, and the son of Lord Hardwicke. He was born on 5 June 1874 and died on 23 December 1943 aged 69.

This photograph was kindly provided by Marsha (Cowen) Garland. Her grandfather, William Martin Cowen, is in the back row, second from the left. He owned a house at 72 Sheringham Gardens, Romford.

The only reference to **William Martin Cowen** is on the British Army First World War medal rolls index cards which shows a William M. Cowen who was a corporal (4726) in the 9th Lancers, which would appear to refer to military service before the First World War. He was then a private S/11836 in the Rifle Brigade and a sapper (112290) in the Royal Engineers. He was awarded the 1915 Star, the British War Medal and the Victory Medal.

Walter arrived in France on 29 June 1915 and was eventually discharged from the army on 17 October 1918 as he was deemed to be no longer fit for war service due to the injuries he had sustained while fighting in France.

One of his sons, Leslie, wrote the following about him:

With the outbreak of World War I on August 4, 1914 he [William Martin Cowen] volunteered and was sent out to France before the end of the month. I believe he had spent some time in the military in South Africa in the 9th Lancers Regiment so was posted to the same regiment then in England.

He subsequently was transferred to the Royal Engineers and was involved in all the major battles in France (the Battle of the Somme, Ypres, etc.) and was severely gassed and wounded in 1917 and was shipped back to England to hospitals there.

Upon his recovery he was posted to a gas experimental station (UK government military science park - site for testing chemical weapons) on the Salisbury Plain (Porton Down) and we lived in the village of Idmiston, Wiltshire until the end of the war and returned to London in early 1919.

Walter Martin Cowen.
(With permission of Marsha Garland)

Although William survived the war he was gassed and wounded while serving in France, injuries which his family feel that he never fully recovered from. He died in 1933.

Marsha's other grandfather also saw service during the First World War. **Charles William Wright** was born in Romford on 8 April 1891 and survived the war despite receiving crippling injuries. He died on 20 December 1939, at the relatively young age of 48. When Marsha's mother was born, Charles was fighting in the trenches in France, hence her mother was christened Frances. Charles had three brothers and a sister, and along with his mother Lizzie they lived at number 40 Waterloo Road in Romford before the war. His father William was still alive and was living in Toronto,

William Martin Cowen.
(Marsha Garland)

Canada. Whether he and Lizzie had separated is not known. One of Charles's brothers, Frank, who was five years younger than him, enlisted in the Canadian army on 17 August 1915 five months short of his nineteenth birthday. He became private 405792 in the 35th Battalion, Canadian Expeditionary Force. No details are known of his wartime service, but he survived the war and stayed in Canada afterwards, marrying Huldah Blanche Silvera from Jamaica in Ontario on 1 September 1923.

In 1917 Balgores House, which is at the northern end of Balgores

Gidea Hall in use as an officers' school for the Artists' Rifles in about 1918.

Lane, and Gidea Hall, were both being used to provide additional accommodation for the Artists Rifles Battalion, which had been offered both properties rent-free by Sir Herbert Raphael.

On the previous page we see Gidea Hall with its windows open, to 'air' it – a typical army touch. Notice if you will the solitary figure of the man leaning on the window sill high up and to the right of the tree. In front of the main entrance it is just possible to make out the bicycles which are parked near a sentry box. The photo is from a postcard sent by a young man who was training at the school. On the reverse he had written the following message:

My dear B & S,

Here is a photo of the school & where I have put the mark is where I sleep & the other is where we dine.

Your loving Brother, George

It is not immediately possible to locate the markings he mentions.

The photograph below shows soldiers marching past Albert Road school in Romford, sometime during the First World War. Note the extremely young-looking officer on the right-hand side of the picture, immediately above the number 4, and the group of young children, playfully following them down the road. The school was built for the Romford School Board in 1883 and opened a year later. It was enlarged in 1890 and again in 1903, and a handicraft centre was opened in 1913.

*Romford, Collier Row & Gidea Park. (*Brian Evans*)*

CHAPTER 4

South Hornchurch Chapel

The names of twenty-four brave young men from the parish who, before going off to fight in the war, were members of the church's congregation each and every Sunday, are commemorated on the South Hornchurch Chapel Roll of Honour, so that those who follow in their footsteps will remember for evermore the ultimate sacrifice that they made.

The chapel was built in 1864 as a church of ease to the Parish Church of St Andrew. The following is taken from *Hornchurch during the Great War* by Charles Thomas Perfect (1921):

On Sunday evening, March 30th, 1919, a special memorial service was held in the Chapel for the twenty-four soldiers and sailors who had died in the war. The Rev. Charles Steer, MC, had arranged to make this the occasion of his first formal visit to the Chapel as Vicar of the Parish, and was to have preached the sermon. He was, however, unfortunately unable to be present, owing to illness; the whole service was therefore taken by Mr Atwood, who also presided at the organ. The chapel was crowded with relatives and friends of the men who had so nobly died for their country, and there were also present many of the men who had been demobilized from active service. Miss Halliday sang from Handel's Messiah, 'I know that my redeemer liveth,' and the Reader in charge took the same beautiful words – John xix, 25-26 for his text, and at the close, the large congregation standing, the Dead March in Saul was played, followed by the reading of the names of the men who had died.

Alfred **Knight**	George **Knight**	Harry **Knight**
Victor Emmanuel **Axup**	Edward **Sargeant**	Richard **Tyler**
Horace Charles **Martin**	George **Chinnery**	Reginald **Bradley**
Alfred Charles **Cook**	Robert **Page**	John **Wilson**
John **Simpson**	Frederick **Doe**	George **Kemp**
William Harry **Thorogood**	William **Abraham**	Ernest **Aylwin**
George William **Cox**	Nathaniel **Hobbs**	George **Wilson**
Alfred Victor **Digby**	John William **Ward**	Ernest Albert **Bennett**

The inscription which is laid out underneath the names reads as follows:

> *These men laid down their lives in the cause of the freedom of their country and of mankind.*

Below, we have taken a look at a few of the names on this roll of honour in a bit more detail, but no offence is inferred to the memories of those of whom we have not mentioned.

Victor Emmanuel **Axup** was a leading signalman in the Royal Navy. He was serving on HMS *Pathfinder* when she was sailing off the Berwickshire coast. She was struck by a torpedo fired by the German U-boat *U-21* and sank, thus becoming the first ship to be sunk by a locomotive torpedo fired from a submarine. HMS *Pathfinder* was a coal-driven vessel, but because of the amount of coal she had on board her speed was reduced to a very slow five knots and she was an easy target for any German submarine or warship in the area. At just before four o'clock in the afternoon, in clear weather, *Pathfinder* was hit by a torpedo on the port side immediately below the bridge. It exploded on contact, setting off one of the ships magazines. There are different estimations as to exactly how many men were on board, but there were only 18 survivors with approximately 250 lost.

> *Despite the events of 5 September having been easily visible from shore, the authorities attempted to cover up the sinking and* Pathfinder *was reported to have been mined. Admiralty came to an agreement with the Press Bureau which allowed for the censoring of all reports.* The Scotsman *however published an eye-witness account by an Eyemouth fisherman who had assisted in the rescue. The account confirmed rumours that a submarine had*

been responsible, rather than a mine. However, The Scotsman *also reported that* Pathfinder *had been attacked by two U-Boats and had accounted for the second one in her death throes. Admiralty intelligence later claimed that cruisers had cornered the U-Boat responsible and shelled it to oblivion. (Wikipedia)*

George **Knight** lived at *The Good Intent* public house in Abbs Cross Road, South Hornchurch, Essex and, according to the 1911 census, he was 19 years of age. He was single and worked as a flooder on a local sewage farm.

Horace Charles **Martin** was a private in the 11th Battalion of the Essex Regiment and 19 years of age when he was killed in action on 22 April 1917 in fighting in and around the area of Loos. His battalion lost a total of sixty-one men. His name is commemorated for evermore on the Loos War Memorial, Pas-de-Calais, which has the names of some 20,000 officers and men who fell in the surrounding areas and who have no known grave. By the time the Commonwealth War Graves Commission began compiling its records in the early 1920s, Horace's parents, Horace Charles (Senior) and Amelia Jane Martin, lived at number 9, Blewitt's Cottages, Rainham.

John William **Ward** was a private (TR10/66259) in the 105th Training Reserve before he transferred to the 648th Agricultural Company Labour Corps where he became private 430523. He was killed on 6 November 1918 aged 24. He is buried at St Andrew's Churchyard, Hornchurch. He left behind a wife, Mrs J.E. Ward, who after his death became Mrs Ainsworth and she lived at number 33 Princes Park, South Hornchurch.

There are an incredible forty-one officers and men who fell during the war buried at St Andrew's Churchyard.

Alfred Victor **Digby** was a private (492830) in the 161st Company, Machine Gun Corps, who along with the 158th, 159th, 160th, 162nd and 163rd Companies, arrived in Egypt in March 1916. In November 1915 the machine gun sections were withdrawn from each of the infantry battalions that they had previously been a part of and formed into machine gun companies which were then attached to each infantry brigade. Hence the birth of the Machine Gun Corps as a separate entity came about, with its very own training centre at Grantham in Lincolnshire. Alfred was killed on 7 December 1917 at the age of 30

St Andrew's Church, Hornchurch. **(Photograph from Church website)**

and is buried in the Damascus Commonwealth War Cemetery in Syria. His wife Florence Lilly lived at Crawford's Cottages, South Hornchurch.

Ernest Albert **Bennett** was a private (177808) in the 1st Battalion,

Canadian Infantry. He was killed in action on 9 July 1916 during the early days of the Battle of the Somme. He has no known grave and his name is commemorated on the Ypres (Menin Gate) War Memorial. His mother, Mrs J. Harriss, lived at Blewitt's Cottages, Rainham, Essex, while his wife, Mary, lived at 89 Parthenais Street, Montreal, Canada.

George William **Cox** was a private (31284) in the 13th Battalion, Essex Regiment, who were also known as the West Ham PALS. He was killed on 30 November 1917.

Ernest Peter **Aylwin** was born in Rainham in 1889. He had a younger brother, Robert, and together they lived with their parents Peter and Alice at 34 Blewitt's Cottages, South Hornchurch. According to the 1911 census, Ernest was single and worked as an agricultural labourer. On 19 September 1914 he married Daisy Ellen Rayment, a spinster, at Romford registry office and they moved in together at number 49 Sheridan Road, Manor Park. Their son, Ernest Frederick, was born on 18 April 1915 at Westham. Ernest Peter enlisted at Eastham on 21 December 1915 and became a private (65473). There is quite a bit of confusion on his attestation form. It originally spells his surname as Aylin but it is subsequently crossed out and respelt Aylwin. He is originally shown as having being allocated to the Kings Royal Rifles, but then that is crossed out and replaced with the Machine Gun Corps, 208th Company. He did in fact serve with the Kings Royal Rifles for two months from 15 August 1916 when he mobilized, until 19 October 1916 when he transferred to the Machine Gun Corps. Although the 208th Company is shown as having deployed to France in June 1918, Ernest is reported as 'missing' from 3 May 1917, but he is shown as having deployed to France on 26 February, the very day he was transferred to the 208th Company from a service company. Further down the same page of his service record there is an entry that says, 'Died on or since 3 May 1917.' In January 1918 Ernest Aylwin is reported as 'Missing' and his wife is awarded a pension of 18/9 a week for her and their son, with effect from 7 January 1918. By June 1918 Daisy Aylwin has moved to Crown Street, Dagenham.

George **Kemp** was a battery sergeant major (14719) with the 99th Siege Battery, Royal Garrison Artillery, and died of his wounds on 28 June 1918. He was born in Romford in 1877. He was awarded the 1915 Star, the British War Medal and the Victory Medal. He is buried at the

Aire Communal Cemetery in the Pas-de-Calais region of France, which has the graves of 894 Commonwealth soldiers buried there. Kemp is also commemorated on the Romford War Memorial. After the war his wife Sophia was living at Clifton House, Gosport Road, Fareham, Hampshire.

Aire Communal Cemetery. **(Commonwealth War Graves Commission)**

The 1911 census shows only one person by the name of John **Simpson** living in the South Hornchurch area and, even he was a lodger, home on leave from the army. He was 21 years of age, having been born in Poplar in 1890, and at the time of the census was lodging with Walter Crabb and his family who lived at number 1, Ivy Cottages, Victory Road, South Hornchurch. Unfortunately there is no indication as to what regiment he was serving with. Having checked the 1901 census there are 2,775 potential matches for the name John Simpson, but not one of them is shown as having been born in Poplar in 1890 in line with the entry above from the 1911 census. Having then checked the British Army Service Records for the period 1914-20, there are 391 possible matches for John Simpson, but out of all of these there was only one who had any obvious connection with the Hornchurch or Romford area.

John Howard **Simpson** was 44 years of age when he enlisted in the army on 25 August 1915 in London and became a sapper (117657) in the Royal Engineers. Before the war he had been a carpenter and lived at 176 Parkhurst Road, Manor Park, Essex, with his wife Mary Ann whom he had married on 29 November 1899 in Islington, and their five children, three sons and two daughters. The day after he enlisted he was promoted to the rank of corporal. Two months later, on 20 October 1915, he was further promoted to the rank of pioneer. What was really surprising in John's case was that less than two weeks after he had enlisted, on 3 September 1915, he was already serving in France, even though he had no previous military experience. He was awarded the 1915 Star, the British War Medal and the Victory Medal, but had been medically discharged from the army on 19 July 1917 for no longer being fit for war service. He had been hospitalized between 7 April and 7 May 1917 (name of hospital not shown). The following was written in the remarks column: 'Complained of breathlessness, palpitation's and pain in left side of head and left side as well…' (The rest of what is written is not legible). This one episode was deemed to have been so severe that it resulted in his almost immediate medical discharge from the army. We have not been able to establish the exact date of when he died, but we already know of the memorial service which was held at the South Hornchurch Chapel to commemorate the twenty-four young men from the parish who had perished during the First World War, on 30 March 1919, and we also know that John Simpson is one of those who is named on the roll of honour. This would also strongly suggest that the reason John Simpson was discharged from the army for being no longer fit for war service was the same illness from which he ultimately died.

The Commonwealth War Graves Commission website comes up with 392 possible matches for John Simpson. When narrowed down to those who served with the Royal Engineers that is then reduced to only nine. None of them have the service number of 117657. One of the nine died on 27 February 1919 and another on 16 May 1920, but neither of them is a match for the John Simpson we were looking for.

William **Abrahams** is the name which is shown on the Hornchurch Roll of Honour as it appears in Charles Perfect's book *Hornchurch in the Great War*. With this information to hand we tried to research William but, despite our best efforts, we couldn't find anything about him other than what had been included in Charles Perfect's book, which said that he served in Egypt with the 4th Battalion, Essex Regiment, and that he was reported as missing. We then searched the list of soldiers from the Essex Regiment who died in the First World War and discovered that William's surname wasn't spelt **Abrahams** but **Abrams**. He was a private (200335) in the 4th Battalion, Essex Regiment, and was killed on 27 March 1917 and that his name is commemorated on the Jerusalem War Memorial along with those of 3,300 others.

At the outbreak of the war, Palestine, which is now Israel, was part of the then Turkish Empire. Allied forces didn't reach there until December 1916, but it would be another year before the Turkish forces holding Jerusalem surrendered and handed the city over to the Egyptian Expeditionary Force, which included the 53rd, 60th and 74th Divisions of the British Army.

Jerusalem War Memorial. **(Commonwealth War Graves Commission)**

The Jerusalem War Memorial was unveiled on 7 May 1927 by Lord Allenby and Sir James Parr.

A search for George **Chinnery** on the Commonwealth War Graves Commission website comes back with no matches whatsoever. A search on the 1911 census shows thirty-four possible matches for the same name, but only one of them came up as living within the Romford district. He lived at number 3, Roger's Cottages, Melville Road, Rainham. He was married to Hannah, who had been his wife for seven years and they had no children. By this time George was already 37 years of age, a potman at a local pub, and Hannah was 41. The British Army First World War medal rolls index shows five individuals with the name George Chinnery. One was in the Rifle Brigade, two in the Labour Corps (although one of these had previously been in the Kings Own Yorkshire Light Infantry), one in the Royal Garrison

ON THIS WALL ARE RECORDED THE NAMES OF OFFICERS AND MEN OF THE ARMIES OF THE UNITED KINGDOM INDIA AND SOUTH AFRICA WHO FELL IN EGYPT AND PALESTINE IN THE GREAT WAR 1914-1918 AND WHO HAVE NO KNOWN GRAVES

(Commonwealth War Graves Commission)

Artillery, and one in the Manchester Regiment but who had started out in the Army Service Corps. Unfortunately we cannot definitively pinpoint which one of them, if any, is the same George Chinnery who we were researching.

Alfred Charles **Knight** was a private (26719) in the 10th Battalion, Essex Regiment, when he was killed in action on 8 March 1917. He is buried in the Queen's Cemetery, Bucquoy, Pas-de-Calais.

Queen's Cemetery, Bucquoy. **(Commonwealth War Graves Commission)**

The village of Bucquoy was wrestled from the Germans' grasp in March 1917 which was when the cemetery began, but was then partly lost just over a year later in April 1918, despite a determined and heroic defence by the 37th, 42nd and 62nd divisions of the British army.

Edward George Thomas **Sargent** enlisted at Ilford as a Trooper (1909) in the Household Battalion of the Household Cavalry and Cavalry of the Line (Including Yeomanry and Imperial Camel Corps). He was 20 years of age when he was killed on 10 October 1917 while serving in Belgium. He had previously served as a private in the Norfolk Yeomanry. His parents, Thomas and Ellen, lived at 7 Bretons Farm, South Hornchurch, with Edward being their only son and child. His name is commemorated on the Tyne Cot War Memorial. There are nearly 35,000 Commonwealth names commemorated on the Tyne Cot War Memorial which was unveiled on 20 June 1927 by Sir Gilbert Dyer.

Tyne Cot War Memorial.
(Commonwealth War Graves Commission)

Alfred Charles **Cook** was a private (27613) in the 3rd Battalion, Northamptonshire Regiment. He died at home on 4 September 1916 from his wounds. He was the son of Hart Spirling and Francis Cook, and is buried at Fort Pitt Cemetery near Maidstone in Kent.

There are 265 graves in the Fort Pitt cemetery of British soldiers who died as a result of fighting during the First World War.

Parents Frederick and Eliza Ann Doe, lived at 15 Baker's Cottage, Abbs Cross, South Hornchurch, Essex and at the time of the First World War they had six sons:

Frederick George **Doe** Private (24592), 9th Battalion Essex Regiment, killed in action 19 July 1917, 23 years of age, born in Hornchurch and enlisted at Upminster. He was a farm labourer before the war.

Brother Alfred James **Doe** served with Royal West Kent Regiment (22566) and survived the war. He had also served with the 2nd/20th

Fort Pitt Cemetery. **(Commonwealth War Graves Commission)**

London Regiment (635051) and the Royal Sussex Regiment (G/32590). Born 6 April 1898, he died June 1979 aged 81 in Havering.

William John **Doe** served as a private (46342) in the Northumberland Fusiliers, saw action in France, and was wounded in the left leg.

Three younger brothers, George Ernest, Arthur Edward, and Frank Charles, were all too young to have served.

Nathaniel **Hobbs** has proved to be somewhat of an elusive character to find. A check on the Commonwealth War Graves Commission website shows two men with the name of Norman Hobbs and one with just N. Hobbs, who was a private (34195) serving with the Royal Gloucestershire Hussars Yeomanry and who was killed on 16 October 1918 in Palestine. A similar check on ancestry.co.uk showed up a Nathaniel Hobbs who had served in the same regiment which was part of the Household Cavalry with the same service number, and who had died on the same date and in the same location. He was born in Silvertown, West Ham, and lived at Fulham Cross. This is as near to finding the exact identity of the Nathaniel Hobbs who is commemorated on the South Hornchurch Chapel Roll of Honour as we could get, although we are still unclear as to where the connection with South Hornchurch came from.

A check for the name Richard **Tyler** on the 1911 census comes up with ninety-six possible matches, but only one of them was living in and had been born in Hornchurch. He was a Richard George Tyler, who the census showed to be a 14-year-old farm hand living at number 1, Bonnet's Cottages, South Hornchurch. He had three younger brothers, William, Thomas and Alfred, along with a sister, Lilly. His parents were Richard and Elizabeth. A search of the Commonwealth War Graves Commission website shows a Richard George Tyler whose parents were Richard and Elizabeth Tyler of South Hornchurch. He was a private (200353) in the 1st/4th Battalion, Essex Regiment, which was a Territorial unit, when he was killed on 27 March 1917. His battalion had been part of the Egyptian Expeditionary Force that had attacked and surrounded Gaza at the end of March 1917 in the First Battle of Gaza, but it was to be of no avail due to the intervention of Turkish reinforcements. It was during this fighting that Private Richard Tyler was killed. He is buried at the Gaza War Cemetery.

Reginald **Bradley** was a private (17049) Royal Marines Light Infantry on board HMS *Hawke* when she was sunk on 15 October 1914 by the German submarine *U-9*. Launched on 11 March 1891, *Hawke* was one of nine Edgar-class cruisers that had been ordered by the Royal Navy as a result of the Naval Defence Act of 1899. She had been given some impressive firepower in the form of twelve six-pounder and four three-pounder guns, which helped provide the ship with anti-torpedo defences. She also had two 9.2-inch guns, ten 6-inch guns, as well as four 18-inch torpedo tubes. In August 1901, when already 20 years old, she was placed in the Navy's Fleet Reserve at Chatham, but six months later she was used to take relief crews to the Cape of Good Hope Station, which was a strategic location used heavily by the British Royal Navy. In November 1904 she started life as a boys' training ship as part of the 4th Cruiser Squadron, then in August 1906 she joined the torpedo training school at Sheerness in Kent, and a year later she joined the Home Fleet. She had her fifteen minutes of fame when on 20 September 1911 she was involved in a collision with the White Star passenger liner RMS *Olympic* which, although only causing minor damage to the latter, resulted in the total loss of *Hawke*'s bow. By now she was 30 years old, but rather than scrap her, as may have been considered, she was repaired and returned back into service.

HMS **Hawke. (Wikipedia)**

After her repairs had been completed, in February 1913, she was on the move once again, this time to Queenstown (now known as Cobh) in Ireland where she joined a training squadron. At the outbreak of the First World War in August 1914 the training squadron was renamed the 10th Cruiser Squadron and was tasked with carrying out blockade duties between the Shetland Islands off Scotland and Norway. On 15 October 1914 HMS *Hawke*, along with the rest of the cruiser squadron, was on patrol off Aberdeen. At 10.30 that morning, *Hawke* was hit by a single torpedo which had been fired by the German submarine *U-9*, causing her to quickly capsize. A total of 542 officers and men on board the *Hawke*, including Reginald Bradley, were killed. Forty-nine survivors were found in a lifeboat by a Norwegian steamer, and a raft with a further twenty-two men was found by the British Naval Destroyer HMS *Swift*.

George **Wilson** was one of the twenty-four names commemorated on the South Hornchurch Chapel Roll of Honour. A check of the 1911 census shows a 17-year-old George Stanley **Wilson** living at number 8, Blewitt's Cottages, South Hornchurch. Before the war he worked as a farm labourer, while his elder brother John Thomas was a 25-year-old factory worker. His other brother, Albert Timothy, was a waterside labourer, which I think might be another way of describing a dock worker.

Checking on UK soldiers who died in the First World War, we discovered a George Stanley **Wilson**, who was born in Rainham, Essex and was a private (27871) in the 1st Battalion, Northamptonshire Regiment. He was killed in action in France on 10 November 1917 and his name is commemorated on the Tyne Cot War Memorial in Zonnebeke, Belgium, which records the names of those who were killed in the area during the war and who have no known grave.

The difficultly of identifying whether John Thomas Wilson had served in the Armed Forces during the First World War with any degree of certainty was highlighted somewhat when we entered his name on the Commonwealth War Graves Commission website only to discover that it came up with 1,038 possible matches. As his name isn't included on the roll of honour for the South Hornchurch Chapel we had initially and understandably assumed that even if he had served during the war, then he had survived.

John Thomas **Wilson** died of the wounds he sustained while serving in France on 3 September 1918. He had been a private (G/22997) in the 7th Battalion, The Queens (Royal West Surrey) Regiment. He is buried in the Barking (Rippleside) Cemetery along with seventy-two other British military personnel who died during the First World War. He had previously served as Private (016230) with the Royal Army Ordnance Corps.

Albert Timothy **Wilson** was older than George but younger than John, so it is inconceivable that he didn't serve his king and country during the First World War, as both of his brothers had. We have searched the British Army First World War medal roll cards, Army Service records, Army Pension records, as well as lists of those killed during the First World War, none of which came up with a direct match. So it would appear that one of the Wilsons sons thankfully survived the war.

CHAPTER 5

Harold Wood Roll of Honour

Records show that there were just over 200 brave young men from Harold Wood who enlisted in His Majesty's Armed Forces and went off to fight in the First World War. When the fighting had come to an end, 26 of them had been killed or died of their injuries, a further 140 of them had safely returned home, and another 40 were still serving in the Forces.

Those who stayed behind, mainly the women, did their bit as well. In the 1911 census, the entire population of Harold Wood was only 1,100, meaning that the community had to make do with a reduction of nearly a fifth of its entire population when some of its menfolk went off to fight in the war. Jobs which had previously been done by men were now being carried out by members of the village's fairer sex. Such jobs included the local postal delivery service, labouring on farms, and work in nearby munitions factories.

During the war years, very few soldiers were ever billeted in Harold Wood, simply because

ROLL OF HONOUR

IN MEMORY OF THE FALLEN
1914.   1919.

W. BARBER.	P. HAYWARD.
C.J. BEARD.	C.T. KING.
E.D. BROWN.	J. LITTLE.
H. CLYDE.	P. LIVERMORE.
A.C. CREEK.	W.A. MARTIN.
R.J. CROW.	F.L. MATTHEWS.
W.S. D'AETH.	J. PETO.
H.G. DIX.	W.H. TAYLOR.
W. FITZJOHN.	E.S. TURNER.
E.A. GARRETT.	W.A. WARMAN.
E. GREEN.	A.S. WARREN.
L. GROUT.	J.W.G. WHITE.
W.F. GUY.	C.W. LITTLE.

"THEY BEING DEAD YET SPEAK."

Roll of Honour. **(Sean Connolly)**

there was never any need to have them staying in the town. It wasn't a strategic location and it didn't have any military establishments in its midst, although there was the aircraft station at nearby Hall Lane in Upminster Common, which was the reason in September 1917 why a small number of soldiers from the Royal Engineers visited the village to connect the village by telephone to the airfield.

Just like towns and villages up and down the country, Harold Wood looked at the best possible way to commemorate the names of its menfolk who had paid the ultimate price and given their lives for king, country and their local community. For them it was not to be a large marble-shaped cross or an obelisk statue, but a rejuvenated and well-equipped entertainments hall – something useful, from which the entire community could benefit. Either side of the entrance doors to the hall are two memorial stones, but unusually they are not inside the hall but on the outside the building and therefore open to the elements and all of the hazards which come with that. On the left-hand side of the main doors as one looks at the front of the building there is the dedication stone, and on the other side is the roll of honour with the names of all twenty-six young men who were killed during the First World War:

W **Barber**	J C S **Beard**	E D **Brown**
H **Clyde**	A C **Creek**	R J **Crow**
W S **D'Aeth**	H G **Dix**	W **Fitzjohn**
E A **Garrett**	E **Green**	L **Grout**
W F **Guy**	P **Hayward**	C T **King**
C W **Little**	J **Little**	P **Livermore**
W A **Martin**	F L **Matthews**	J **Peto**
W H **Taylor**	E S **Turner**	W A **Warman**
A S **Warren**	J W G **White**	

The dedication stone has the following words engraved on it, although it is now in need of some minor repair:

Dedicated at the end of the Great War, 1914-1919, by the inhabitants of Harold Wood, in grateful commemoration of the glorious heroism and high sense of duty of all those who served in the sea, land and air forces, and in loving memory of those who made the great sacrifice.

The memorial stones were unveiled in a ceremony which took place on Saturday, 15 November 1919, performed by Mr Edward Bryant, a local JP. He had also been the previous owner of the hall and had generously handed the hall over to the memorial committee free of charge as his contribution to the memorial fund. The prayers at the service were read out by the Reverend B. Hartley MA.

THE
HAROLD WOOD
MORIAL INSTITUTE

EDICATED AT THE END
F THE GREAT WAR
14 — 1919 BY THE
HABITANTS OF HAROLD
OOD IN GRATEFUL
OMMEMORATION OF
E GLORIOUS HEROISM
HIGH SENSE OF DUTY
F ALL THOSE WHO
RVED IN THE SEA
     AIR FORCES
         AND IN
         MORY OF
OSE WHO MADE THE
GREAT SACRIFICE.

(Photograph Sean Connolly)

The unveiling ceremony attracted a large and enthusiastic crowd of local parishioners, friends, and relatives of the deceased servicemen, who laid wreaths and other flower tributes at the foot of the memorial stones, after which the *Last Post* was played by a lone bugler.

Arthur Charles **Creek** was born in Canning Town in 1899. He was an able seaman (Z/2950) in the Royal Naval Volunteer Reserve, serving on board HMS *Partridge*, having joined the Royal Navy in August 1915. He was killed on 12 December 1917 when his ship was sunk, along with all but twenty-two of the crew. He was 20 years of age. Along with four of his colleagues who also perished that day, he is buried at the Fredrikstad Military Cemetery in Norway.

HMS *Partridge* was part of the Grand Fleet of the British Navy and involved in the daily convoys of merchant shipping that travelled the seas between Lerwick in Scotland and Bergen in Norway. On 11 December 1917 one such convoy left Lerwick; it was made up of six merchant ships which were being escorted by six Royal Navy vessels of the Grand Fleet. The first indication of any trouble came at around 1130 hours when the convoy, approaching the coast of Norway, spotted four German torpedo boats, that were under the command of Lieutenant Colonel Kolbe, bearing down on them. It was a cold and overcast day, which wasn't unusual for December in the North Sea. Matters were not helped by the heavy rain and rough seas. During the ensuing engagement HMS *Partridge*, along with the rest of the convoy except for HMS *Pellew*, was sunk with the loss of 5 officers and 92 men. The rest of the crew, 3 officers and 21 men, were picked up by the Germans and taken prisoner.

Arthur Ernest **Creek** was the cousin of Arthur Charles Creek. The latter's mother was the sister of Arthur Ernest's father. A.E. Creek finished the war as a sergeant (52353) in the Royal Field Artillery, finally being demobbed in February 1919. He was awarded the 1915 Star, the British War Medal, the Victory Medal and the Military Medal, the citation of which read as follows:

> *Awarded the Military Medal for courage and devotion to duty on 6 June 1918 when he remained at his post during a violent bombardment and although suffering from the effects of gas shelling, he continued, with the help of a comrade, to fire his gun in response to an SOS call.*

Ernest Albert **Garrett** was born in Takely in the north of Essex in 1895. His elderly parents, George and Emma, were, according to the 1911 census, 85 and 63 years of age. Ernest had two elder brothers, Charles Henry, was born in 1884, and Robert Thomas, born in 1886. Along with George's brother William, who was, according to the 1911 census, 80 years of age, the family lived at number 1, Maria Cottage, Harold Wood. By the time that the Commonwealth War Graves Commission had started compiling its records, in the early 1920s, Ernest was shown as having been married to Gertie, their home being at number 1, St John Cottage, Queens Park Road, Harold Wood. He was a corporal (G/34048) in the 17th Battalion, Middlesex Regiment, when he was killed on 28 April 1917 during the Arras Offensive which took place between April and May that year. His name is commemorated on the Arras War Memorial in the Pas-de-Calais. There are 35,000 names on the memorial of servicemen, from the United Kingdom, New Zealand and South Africa, who were killed in the Arras area between April 1916 and 7 August 1918 and who have no known grave. It's not known with any degree of certainty whether or not either of Ernest's brothers served in the military during the First World War. If they did, then they survived, as they are not shown as having been fatalities of the war.

William Samuel **D'Aeth** was born in Harold Wood, lived in Ingatestone, and enlisted in Chelmsford, where he became a private (G/24979) in the 3rd/4th Battalion, Queens (Royal West Surrey) Regiment. He was killed in action on 7 October 1917 while serving on the Western Front in France. He had previously served as a private

(241933) with the East Kent Regiment. William's name is commemorated on the Tyne Cot War Memorial. There is also a Tyne Cot Cemetery on the same site which was established around a captured German pill-box. It is the largest Commonwealth war cemetery in the world with the graves of 11,956 servicemen from the First World War. Of these, 8,369 are unidentified. The spelling of William's surname is unusual; more normally this name is spelt D'Eath. On the British Army First World War medal roll cards his surname is spelt as **Daith**, and it is definitely the same person.

If you enter W. **Fitzjohn** into the search engine of the Commonwealth War Graves Commission website, there are four possible matches. The most likely match is Walter Charles Fitzjohn. He was born in Brentwood, lived in Hornchurch, and enlisted at Romford where he became private 19226 in the 2nd Battalion, Essex Regiment. He was killed in action on 3 May 1917 and is commemorated on the Arras War Memorial in the Pas-de-Calais region of France.

Arras War Memorial and Cemetery. **(Commonwealth War Graves Commission)**

His wife, Emma Fitzjohn, lived at Wells Cottages, Aldleigh Green, Hornchurch. Walter had five brothers, William, Frederick, Robert, Harry, and Bertie.

Robert Frank **Fitzjohn** was a private (52333) in the 1st Battalion,

Royal Scots Regiment. He had enlisted way back on 5 December 1894 at Warley, when only having just turned 18 years of age, signing on for twelve years. This was twenty years before the First World War had even begun. Before enlisting in the Royal Scots, Robert had previously served with the 4th Battalion, Essex Regiment, which was a Territorial unit, or as it was then referred to, a Militia. On 17 April 1902 he was admitted to hospital in Poona, India suffering from a 'contusion' which 'may possibly result in a permanent disability and may affect his future efficiency as a soldier.' Luckily for Robert this would appear not to have been the case. He married Ethel Beatrice Woodward on 3 October 1908 in Essex. They had two children while Robert was serving in India, one of whom died of disease at a very young age. After having served with the Royal Scots for eighteen years and seventy-one days, Robert Frank Fitzjohn, having reached the rank of corporal, decided it was time to retire, knowing that by doing so before he had reached twenty-one years' service his pension would be reduced by twenty-five percent of its total value from what it would have been if he had stayed on. He was now 36 years of age and the date was 7 March 1913. It would appear that he spent a period of time in the military working as what would today be known as a physical education instructor, a roll that he was looking to continue on leaving the army, but in a school environment where he could pass his skills and knowledge on to children. Seventeen months later, on 19 October 1914, Robert re-enlisted in the army at Warley, where he had first joined up twenty years earlier. Initially he served as a private (239968) with the 3rd Battalion, Essex Regiment, and within a month of enlisting he found himself in France, arriving there on 24 November 1914. Four months later, on 17 March 1915, he returned to England where he would spend the rest of the war. He later transferred to the Bedfordshire Regiment on 27 March 1917, before again transferring, this time to the Labour Corps on 28 August 1917. He was demobbed on 24 February 1919, having served for the entire period of the war bar two months, and having served in the Army for a total of 22 years and 24 days.

Bertie Alfred **Fitzjohn** was the youngest of the six Fitzjohn brothers, being born at Brentwood in 1889. He was attested at Chelmsford on 27 February 1915 and was called up on 15 June 1915 when he joined the 13th Battalion, Middlesex Regiment, and became Private 58418.

He had only been in the army for three months when he received what was to be the only blemish on his personal conduct sheet. He failed to turn up to stable attendant duty. He later transferred to 113 Company, 11th Divisional Training Regiment of the Army Service Corps, although it is not clear from his Army Service record when or why. He had served in Egypt between January and April 1916 and then in Salonica from April 1916 to December 1918. While serving in Salonica he contracted malaria in October 1917 due to the 'climatic conditions'. He was demobbed on 23 February 1919 at Great Baddow in Chelmsford and placed on the Army Reserve.

The best I have been able to come up with on Frederick Alma **Fitzjohn** is that according to the British Army First World War medal rolls index cards there were five men with the same name. Three were in the Royal Garrison Artillery, one in the Royal Army Medical Corps and the other in the Royal Engineers.

No Army service or pension records have survived for any of the Frederick Fitzjohns for us to be able to narrow it down any further.

It's a similar story with William Walter **Fitzjohn**. I have not been able to find any obvious candidates for the one we are looking for, but once again the British Army's First World War medal rolls index cards comes up with five possible matches.

It must have been a traumatic time for the brothers' parents, Benjamin and Emma, having six sons who were all old enough to be called up to serve their king and country.

William Alfred **Warman** began his military service as Private 1361 (200142) in the 4th Battalion, Essex Regiment, which was a Territorial Army unit made up of men who predominantly came from the Hornchurch area of the county. Sometime during the war, he transferred into the Royal Flying Corps, where he became a 2nd lieutenant. The Royal Flying Corps and the Royal Naval Air Service amalgamated on 1 April 1918 to become the Royal Air Force. He enlisted in August 1914 at the very start of hostilities when he was 19 years of age. He was killed on 13 October 1918, less than a month before the end of the war. He is buried at the Cairo War Memorial Cemetery in Egypt.

After the war, those members of the military who qualified for campaign medals had them sent out in the post. This happened in the early 1920s. William's next of kin was shown as his stepmother, Mrs

Emma Cumbers of number 2, Queens Park Road, Harold Wood, Romford. Her husband George Hayden had died in March 1918 at the age of 49. William was awarded the 1915 Star, the British War Medal and the Victory Medal. The 1911 census shows the family lived at number 1, Redden Court Lodge, Harold Wood, and that William had a step-brother, Alfred Thomas Cumbers; they were both 16 years of age at the time.

Cairo War Memorial Cemetery. (Commonwealth War Graves Commission)

Alfred served in the Royal Field Artillery as an acting sergeant (87570) and was awarded both the British War Medal and the Victory Medal. Unlike William, Albert survived the war and lived to the ripe old age of 87, passing away in September 1982. How different life could have been for William if luck had been on his side.

Percy James **Livermore** was a private (1199/200088) in the 1st/4th Battalion, Essex Regiment, when he was killed on 19 September 1918. He was awarded the 1915 Star, the British War Medal and the Victory Medal. He is buried at the Ramleh (now Ramla) War Cemetery in Israel which was started in November 1917 with the arrival of the 1st Australian Light Horse Brigade, which resulted in both field ambulances and later casualty clearing stations being posted to the town.

Ramleh War Cemetery. (Commonwealth War Graves Commission)

There are 3,000 graves of Commonwealth servicemen from the First World War buried in the cemetery; 964 of them are unidentified. Percy's mother, Elizabeth Livermore, lived at number 1, St John's Cottage, Queens Park Road, Harold Wood. He also had an elder brother, Frederick, but we have not been able to establish with any degree of certainty if he served in the military during the First World War, but at his age it is almost inconceivable that he didn't.

W. **Barber's** case is one of the thousands upon thousands of sad stories which inevitably came about as a result of the war. When he enlisted at the very beginning of the war on 6 August 1914 he became a private in the Royal North Lancashire Regiment, but was soon transferred to the Cheshire Regiment where he became Private 29031 of the 13th Battalion. He was shot during the Allied retreat at the Battle of Mons when he received a bullet wound that pierced his right lung. Two years later, and still not having fully recovered from his wounds, he was medically discharged from the army on 27 August 1916 for no longer being physically fit enough for war service. He died on 4 April 1918 of consumption; he was 33 years of age. He is buried in St Andrew's Churchyard, Hornchurch, along with thirty-six other service men who died as a result of their involvement in the First World War.

C.J. **Beard** was a driver (T4/146769) in the Army Service Corps, attached to 1st Battalion, Surrey Yeomanry (Queen Mary's Regiment), when he was killed on 17 October 1918. He is buried at the Mikra British Cemetery in Kalamaria, Greece. French and allied troops were in Greece at the request of the country's Prime Minister, Eleftherios Venzelos, first arriving there in October 1915. The cemetery was first used by Commonwealth forces in November 1915 and received its last burial in October 1918. The cemetery contains the graves of some 1,810 Commonwealth service men, as well another 147 from other Allied countries, who fell victim to the First World War. It also contains the Mikra War Memorial, which commemorates the names of nearly 500 Commonwealth officers, men and nurses, who died when troop transport ships and hospital ships were lost in the Mediterranean.

Mikra British Cemetery, Kalamaria. **(Commonwealth War Graves Commission)**

Ernest Denham **Brown** was a driver (82823) in the 47th Battery, 44th Brigade, Royal Field Artillery, when he died on 28 July 1916. He is buried in the Carnoy Military Cemetery, which is in the Somme region of France; it has some 850 graves of men who fell during the First World War. His parents, Alfred and Amy Brown, lived at Ardleigh Green, Hornchurch, while his wife Kate lived at number 2, Bishop's Cottages, Queens Park Road, Harold Wood, Romford.

The 1911 census showed that he had three sisters and a brother, Bertie Walter Brown, who was only two years younger than him. We have not been able to identify with any degree of certainty which if any regiment Bertie served in during the war, although there is no record of him having being killed.

Harold **Clyde** was a private (82849) in the 2nd Battalion, London Regiment, Royal Fusiliers. Ancestry.co.uk records that he was killed in action on 21 March 1918, but the Commonwealth War Graves Commission website records that he was killed a month later on 24 April 1918. He was 18 years of age. He had previously been a private (39930) in the 3rd Battalion, Bedfordshire Regiment, as well as a Private (52081) in the 12th Battalion, Middlesex Regiment. The 1911 census shows that he lived at Oak Road, Harold Wood, with his parents and four older sisters. He is buried at the Hangard Wood British Cemetery in the Somme region of France which now holds the graves of 141 Commonwealth soldiers from the First World War. Hangard is a village which sits between Domart and Demuin. In the Spring of 1918 it was where French and Commonwealth forces were dug in trying to prevent the German advance towards Amiens. Between 4 and 25 April, both the village of Hangard and the surrounding woods were the scene of some extremely heavy fighting, but the Germans did not break through. It was during this fighting that Private Clyde was killed.

Edward **Green** enlisted in the 13th Battalion, Royal Sussex Regiment on 26 December 1916 and went on to serve in France from 10 March 1917 to 23 March 1918, when he was killed in action. His name is commemorated on the Pozières War Memorial in the Somme. The memorial includes the names of the Allied and Commonwealth soldiers who were killed between March and April 1918 when the 5th Army was driven back across the Somme by overwhelming German forces. It was during this enforced retreat that Edward was killed. He left behind a wife, Lavinia Maud, of 3 Archibald Road, Harold Wood.

Leslie Arthur John **Grout** enlisted in August 1914 and became a sapper (313240) in the Royal Fusiliers before transferring to the 5th Survey Company, Royal Engineers, on 30 March 1917. He was killed on 30 March 1918. Leslie is buried at the Villers-Bretonneux Military Cemetery in the Somme region of France. His mother, Mrs A Grout, lived at Engleside, Harold Wood.

W.F. **Guy** was a private in the 4th Battalion, Essex Regiment, which was a Territorial unit. He served with them in the Gallipoli campaign, arriving there in June 1915, and while serving there was promoted to the rank of corporal. In December 1916 he was sent back to England to have his wounds taken care of. By February 1917 he was fit enough to return to duty and was sent out to Egypt where less than a month later, on 27 March 1917, he was killed in action.

P. **Hayward** enlisted in the Middlesex Regiment on 5 May 1916, before transferring to the 7th Battalion. He was reported missing in action on 28 September 1916.

Charles Thomas **King** was a corporal (18172) in the 1st Battalion, Hampshire Regiment. He enlisted in the army on 3 June 1915 and it would be another nine months before he arrived in France, on 8 March 1916, and four months after that he was dead, falling on the first day of the Battle of the Somme, 1 July 1916. His name is commemorated on the Thiepval war memorial.

John **Little** was a private (7139) in the 3rd Battalion, Royal Fusiliers, and was 19 years of age when he was killed on 24 May 1915. His name is commemorated on the Ypres (Menin Gate) Memorial. His parents, George Shelley and Emma, lived at number 7, Queens Park Road, Harold Wood.

C.W. **Little** was a private (69446) in the 6th Battalion, Royal West Surrey Regiment, having enlisted on 9 January 1918. Sadly, just eight months later, and with Private Little still only 18 years of age, he was

Peronne Communal Cemetery Extension (Photograph Commonwealth War Graves Commission)

dead, killed in action whilst fighting on the Western Front on 21 September. He is buried in the Peronne Communal Cemetery Extension, which is situated in the Somme region of France.

He was the son of Mrs M.A. Little, of Tyler's Hall Farm, Upminster Common.

W.A. **Martin** was a private (238027) in the 1st/4th Battalion, Suffolk Regiment, when he was killed on 26 April 1917. He is buried in the St Sever Cemetery Extension, at Rouen in the Seine-Maritime region of France, which contains a total of 8,348 Commonwealth graves from the First World War.

St Sever Cemetery. (**Commonwealth War Graves Commission**)

Rouen was an important location for Commonwealth and Allied forces during the war. There was a major supply depot situated in the city, along with an army headquarters and numerous different types of hospitals. Martin's parents, Arthur and Mary Ann Martin, lived at number 2, Queens Park Road, Harold Wood.

Frank Lawson **Matthews** was a private (STK/461) in 'B' Company, 10th Battalion, Royal Fusiliers (City of London) Regiment, when he was killed in action on 19 November 1916, aged 21. He was buried in the Varennes Military Cemetery. Varennes village is situated about ten miles away from Amiens.

The cemetery was started in August 1916 by the 39th Casualty Clearing Station during the bloody Battle of the Somme and was continued by the 4th and 11th Casualty Clearing Stations who moved into the area in October 1916. The cemetery contains the graves of 1,219 allied and Commonwealth servicemen who were killed during the First World War.

W.H. **Taylor** enlisted in the army in January 1915 and became a corporal (66247) in the 214th Army Troops Company, Royal Engineers. He was awarded the Meritorious Service Medal while serving in France. He was also a Lewis gun instructor. He died on 26 February 1919, not of gunshot wounds or an artillery bombardment, but of pneumonia. Yet another young life extinguished before its time. He is buried at the Kortrijk (St Jan) Communal Cemetery in the West-Vlaanderen region of Belgium.

Taylor's wife, Mabel Sophie Taylor, lived at 'Thornsette', Harold Wood.

E.S. **Turner** was a lieutenant in the Royal Naval Volunteer Reserve who served on both trawlers and Royal Naval Motor launches in the North Sea and the West Indies throughout the war. Ironically, after surviving the war, it would be his journey back home to England that would be his downfall when he contracted flu and pneumonia. On his arrival home he was admitted to the Fazakerley Hospital in Liverpool where he died not long after, on 6 March 1919. He is buried in the Roby (St Bartholomew) Churchyard in Lancashire. There are two other British servicemen buried in the same churchyard who fell as a result of the First World War.

Arthur Stanley **Warren** was a private (G/11367) in the 2nd Battalion, Royal Fusiliers, when he was killed in the fighting of the Gallipoli campaign on 28 June 1915. His name is commemorated on the Helles War Memorial in Turkey. His mother Emma lived at 32 Pretoria Road, Romford.

Jessie Walter Gordon **White** was a corporal (8193) in the Army Pay Corps. He died on 9 February 1920 aged 33 and is buried at Ilford Cemetery. There are fifty-two British servicemen who served in the First World War buried in the cemetery. The 1911 census shows that

Jessie was a chartered accountant's clerk and was living with his wife Roberta Alice at number 42, Quebec Road, Ilford. He was obviously doing well for himself as he and Roberta employed a servant girl. The National Index of Wills and Administration for England and Wales shows his home address as being Ditton Dene, Station Road, Harold Wood. He died at Albert Hall Military Hospital in Nottingham and in his will he left £433 6s, all of which was left to his wife Roberta.

CHAPTER 6

Romford Cemetery

There are twenty-six young men buried in Romford cemetery who died as a result of their service in the First World War. Only ten of them have Commonwealth War Grave Commission-style headstones on their graves. In most cases that will simply be because the dead man's family would have politely declined the offer. In some cases it will be because of an official oversight where the location or the existence of the dead serviceman's grave is not known.

1914

John Henry **Seymour** was an able seaman (172514) attached to HMS *Pembroke* when he died on 16 December 1914 aged 37. His widow Lily was living at number 16, Margaret Road, Heath Park in Romford, at the time of his death, although before the war they had lived at number 4, Parr's Cottages, Nursery Walk, Romford, with their two children John Harold,10, and Grace Lily Seymour, 5. In 1914 HMS *Pembroke* was a land-based Royal Naval Air Station at Eastchurch on the Isle of Sheppey as well as a Medina-class gunboat. Up until 1905 she had been named HMS *Trent*. There is no record of HMS *Pembroke* having been damaged or sunk on 16 December 1914, although coincidentally that was the same day that the German navy carried out attacks on Scarborough, Whitby and Hartlepool. In the ensuing sea battle, which took place as Royal Navy vessels gave chase, six ratings were killed. It is a possibility that John was attached to one of these ships at the time. There is a record of a casualty from the shore base HMS *Pembroke* at Eastchurch on 16 December 1914, but that was a Petty Officer Lionel Rainsford who died of illness. A check of the records for all naval ratings lost during the First World War does not record John Henry Seymour as a casualty.

1915

James Lambert **Jenkin** was born in Redruth in Cornwall but eventually enlisted and became a private (SR/2664) in the 24th Battalion, Royal Fusiliers. He died of wounds on 15 July 1915. He was 25 years of age. James had a brother, Richard, who was four years older than him, who we could find no trace of having served in the military during the First World War. This could possibly be because the 1911 census showed him as being employed working in the Cornish tin mines. Their parents, Samuel and Mary, lived at The Firs, Scorrier, Cornwall.

Harry **Chater** was a private (M2/101451) in the 341st Motor Transport Company, Army Service Corps, when he died on 5 September 1915. He was 31 years of age. Harry was a local lad. After the war his mother was still living in Romford which, although it was Harry's birthplace, he had already moved out of by the time of the 1911 census. By then he was married to Phoebe and they were living at 62 Cromwell Road in Forest Gate where Harry was a van salesman. The 1891 census shows Harry, who is only 6 years of age at the time, living in Romford with his parents, Charles and Sarah, his three sisters, a cousin, one of his dad's brothers, and his grandfather on his mother's side. By the time of the 1901 census he has left home and is lodging with Mr and Mrs Raddon and their seven children in Walthamstow. Why he had left home and was lodging with another family is not explained. By the time of the 1911 census, Harry's mum Sarah is living on her own at 66 St Andrew's Road, Romford, but she is shown as being a wife rather than a widow.

W.G. **Wakeling** was William George Wakelin, a private (17074) in the 1st Battalion, Essex Regiment. He was born and bred in Romford and enlisted in the army at nearby Warley. William landed at Cape Helles, Gallipoli, with his colleagues from the 1st Battalion on 25 April 1915. After having been wounded during the ferocious fighting against Turkish forces on the peninsula, he was returned to hospital in the United Kingdom, where he died of his wounds on 8 September 1915. He was 35 years of age. His name is commemorated on the Hornchurch War Memorial but has for some inexplicable reason been misspelt so that it reads Wakleing. The 1911 census shows William living at 29 Richmond Road, Romford with his wife Frances and their daughter, Alice, who was 5 years of age. After the war, Francis and Alice left Romford and moved to 3 Ridge Road, Sutton in Surrey.

1916

A. **Wopling** was Arthur Wopling who was a private (24315) in the 6th Battalion, Essex Regiment. He was born in Little Holland, Essex and enlisted at West Ham. The 6th Battalion had been involved in the fighting at Gallipoli having being there in August-December 1915. They then moved on to Mudros and eventually landed in Alexandria in Egypt on 17 December 1915, remaining in the region for the rest of the war. It was while being stationed there that Arthur received his wounds that resulted in him being sent back to hospital in the United Kingdom. He died of his wounds at Sevenoaks Hospital in Kent on 12 March 1916. He was 49 years of age. The 1911 census shows him working as a brewery labourer, a job that a lot of men would have willingly swapped with him

(Photograph Sean Connolly)

because of the obvious perks that went with it. He was living at 49 Waterloo Road, Romford with his wife Eliza and their three children, Amy who was 15, Arthur who was 12, and Elsie who was 9. 1916 was not going to be a good year for Eliza Wopling, because not only did she lose her husband Arthur, she also lost her son, with both of them dying in the month of March.

H.V. **Smart** was Horace Victor Smart, who enlisted in the army at the recruiting office in Bedford three years before the start of the war in October 1911 and became Private (9859) in the 2nd Battalion (16th Foot), Bedfordshire Regiment. He had served in South Africa before becoming part of the British Expeditionary Force in France and Flanders from October 1914. The 1911 census showed the family living at 22 Salisbury Road, Romford, which included Horace's parents, George and Alice, and his two elder brothers, William and Herbert. Horace was 23 years old, single, and a butcher by trade. He died in the Royal Victoria Hospital in Netley, which is near Southampton in Hampshire, on 1 August 1916, from wounds he received while fighting at Metz Woods on12 July. The construction of Netley Hospital began in 1856 at the suggestion of Queen Victoria, opening its doors to patients for the first time on 19 May 1863. It was used extensively throughout the First World War for the medical treatment of soldiers returning from France and Belgium with neurological problems directly connected to the effects of 'shell shock'. There is no trace of Horace on the Commonwealth War Graves Commission website as an individual who was killed during the course of the war. The British Army First World War medal index cards show a Horace V. Smart of the Bedfordshire Regiment. There is some doubt as to whether his army service number was 9859 or 9959. He arrived in France on 6 October 1914 and for his wartime service was awarded the 1914 Star, the British War Medal, and the Victory Medal.

His brother William had not only served as a driver (20331) with the Royal Artillery throughout the whole war – having been mobilized on 5 August 1914 eventually being demobilized on 10 February 1919 – but he had originally enlisted on 30 December 1901 during the time of the Second Boer war. Although the British army medal rolls index cards shows thirty-seven Herbert Smart's we could not find a direct match for Horace and William's brother.

G.J. **Hawkins** was George James Hawkins, a Barking man by birth, who enlisted at Romford. He became a private (26715) in the 10th Battalion, Essex Regiment, and was a holder of the Military Medal, awarded for his gallantry in battle. He died of his wounds on 18 October 1916. He was 28 years of age. The 1991 census shows George as being a general labourer living at 211 Marks Road, Romford, with his two younger brothers, his sister, her husband and their two young children.

G.R. **Murphy** was an air mechanic 1st class in the Royal Naval Air Service. He died on 22 October 1916.

1917

R. **Ramsey** was a private (43365) in the 17th Battalion, Manchester Regiment. He died of his wounds on 18 March 1917. He was 29 years of age.

Linton Albert Ramsey **Fennell** was a private (765361) in the 2nd/28th Battalion, London Regiment, County of London (Artists Rifles). He died of sickness on 14 April 1917. He was 37 years of age. Although he had been attested on 29 November 1915, he wasn't called up until 8 March 1917 and a month later he was dead, dying of scarlet fever in Romford Isolation Hospital. The 1911 census showed that he was born in Plaistow in East London but lived in Bassett Road, Camborne in Cornwall. By profession he was a dentist and lived with Kate Eugenie Williams and her two children, Lorna and Jack. It's surprising that with Linton's medical background he wasn't commissioned as an officer and posted to the Royal Army Medical Corps.

(Photograph Sean Connolly)

R.J. **Palmer** was a private (21232) in the Buffs (East Kent) Regiment. He died on 27 August 1917 aged 27.

Harold **White** was an ordinary seaman (J/61552 (CH)) in the Royal Navy. He was killed on 6 September 1917 aged 22.

John Joseph **Shearman** was a private (SR 3/10398) in H Company, 3rd Battalion, Norfolk Regiment, before he transferred to 581 HSE Company, Labour Corps, as Private 287083. He was killed in an accident on 2 November 1917, the details of which are not known. His widow, Alice Phoebe, lived at 40 Milton Road in Romford.

1918

S.E. **Saunders** was Sydney Edgar Saunders, born in Romford, and enlisted in the town as well. He was Private (200181) who joined the 4th Battalion, Essex Regiment, which was a Territorial unit whose men predominantly came from the Romford, Hornchurch, Upminster and Barking areas, which gave it a sort of pals battalion feeling.

(Photograph Sean Connolly)

Ernest Charles **Disney** was a driver (102979) in the 6th Division Ammunition Column, Royal Field Artillery. He was 25 years of age when he died on 19

February 1918 in hospital in Exeter from wounds he had received while fighting in France. The town was awash with military establishments at the time, with seven VAD hospitals alone. The 1911 census showed the Disney family living at number 33 Cotleigh Road, Romford. Mum and dad were Mary and Ernest Disney, then there were their three sons, Ernest who was the oldest, followed by William who was 17, and Edward Mortimer who was 13. Ruth Mary Disney, the baby of the family, was 2 years old. We can find no trace of either William or Edward having served their country during the First World War. Ernest was already 18 at the time of that year's census and working as a shop assistant in one of the town's shops.

(Photograph Sean Connolly)

Alexander **Clarke** was a major in the 7th (Queens Own) Hussars. He was killed on 2 August 1918. He was 51 years of age.

Edwin Valentine **French** was a flight cadet in the Royal Air Force. He was killed on 16 October 1918. He was 18 years of age.

(Photograph Sean Connolly)

J.E. **Currie** was a flight cadet in the Royal Air Force when he died, on 26 October 1918.

Charles Ernest **Phillips**, having enlisted in the county town of Chelmsford, became a rifleman (TR13/84254) in the 10th Battalion, Rifle Brigade. At the time of his death, on 16 October 1918, he had been serving with the Regiment's 53rd Battalion. He was only 18 years of age. The Phillips family lived at 3 Margaret Road in Romford. Charles's father John Henry had died a year before the outbreak of the war, on 4 August 1913. His mother Emma died on 27 December 1946. Both are remembered on Charles's Commonwealth War Graves Commission headstone at Romford Cemetery. There is a slight anomaly, as on the headstone Charles's father's name is recorded as being John Charles Phillips, yet on his birth certificate and in the 1911 census his name is clearly shown as being John Henry; but we are happy that both entries relate to the same person.

Charles had three brothers, John Henry, who was 23 years of age at the time of the 1911 census, James Bernard, who was 14 and little Horace who was 3. His sister Ethel was 5.

(Photograph Sean Connolly)

Both John and William would have been old enough to have served their country during the First World War, but we have been unable to find an exact match for either of them having actually done so.

P.J. **Moore** was originally a gunner (155305) in the Royal Field Artillery before transferring to the Labour Corps where he became a lance corporal (314190). He died on 14 November 1918, sadly just three days after the end of the war.

(Photograph Sean Connolly)

1919

D. **Haley** was a company sergeant major (3/9899) in the West Yorkshire Regiment (Prince of Wales's Own). He was killed on 29 January 1919. He was 40 years of age.

A.G. **Rich** was a private (R/445925) in the Remount Depot, Royal Army Service Corps. He died on 22 March 1919. His father, Alfred Rich, lived at 61 Market Place, Romford.

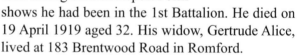

S. **Robison** was a private (513138). The Commonwealth War Graves Commission website shows that he was in the 14th Battalion, London Regiment (London Scottish), but the actual Graves Registration Report Form shows he had been in the 1st Battalion. He died on 19 April 1919 aged 32. His widow, Gertrude Alice, lived at 183 Brentwood Road in Romford.

(Photograph Sean Connolly)

(Photograph Sean Connolly)

Horace **Hilton** was a private in the City of London Yeomanry (Rough Riders). He was killed on 6 May 1919. He was 22 years of age.

W.J. **Salmons** was originally a private (6269) in the 21st Battalion, East of India Lancers, before he transferred, at the same rank of private, to the Labour Corps.

1921

S.W. **Steward** was a private (5998205) in the Essex Regiment. He was demobilized on 19 March 1921.

(Photograph Sean Connolly)

CHAPTER 7

The Six **Bill** Brothers of Romford

During the First World War there weren't many families throughout Great Britain that weren't affected in some way or another by the loss of a loved one, or of a close friend who had been killed or died as a result of the horrors of four years of bloody war. Villages and towns back then were tight-knit communities where everybody knew each other and the church played a central role in daily life.

When a young man from one of these communities became a casualty of the war, everybody felt the loss and the pain. Family, friends, and neighbours would have known the young man concerned, and like him would have probably been born, baptised and lived in the same community all of their lives.

Most families felt that pain through the loss of a husband or a son. Some might have been unlucky enough to experience the loss of two loved ones. Some families had to deal with the loss of a lot more.

William Thomas Bill, a wool merchant, and his wife Selina, had six sons, all of whom served in the First World War. In the 1911 census his parents show as living at 'The Cottage', Havering Well, Hornchurch Road, Romford.

Charles Smith **Bill** was a private (426471) in the 3rd Battalion, Canadian Infantry when he died on 13 June 1916. He was 22 years of age having been born on 7 June 1894. His name is commemorated on the Ypres Menin Gate war memorial in Belgium. The 3rd Canadian Division had been in Belgium since the end of March 1916 but it wouldn't be until 1 June that they were involved in their first battle with the Germans who had launched an offensive at Mont Sorrel and the areas that were known locally as Hills 61 and 62, which were also known as Sanctuary Wood. The Germans won the day, pushed the Canadians back, and took control of the entire area. The following day saw the Canadians mount an unsuccessful counter-attack to win back Mont Sorrel and Hills 61 and 62. On 13 June the Canadians launched a swift and well-prepared offensive against the Germans which consisted of a heavy and accurate artillery bombardment, followed by a swift and immediate infantry assault that was so well coordinated, the Canadian troops arrived at the German trenches just as the artillery barrage stopped. So well was the plan executed that all of the lost ground was retaken, but it came at a price. The Canadians suffered a total of 8,430 casualties. Charles Smith Bill was one of them.

Charles and his younger brother Arthur emigrated to Canada sailing on board the Allan Line vessel *Corinthian*. They arrived in Montreal on 5 June 1913 having left London on 8 May. The 1911 census shows that Charles, who was 16 years of age at the time, was a student in a cloth mill. The entry for 'trade or profession' on the passenger list for when he arrived in Canada was 'farming'. Sometime after having arrived in Canada, and with the war in Europe now underway, Charles and Arthur decided to enlist in the army and to do their bit for the king and Commonwealth. They both joined the 3rd Battalion, Canadian Infantry Regiment, and ended up serving in France.

Frank Keen **Bill** was a private (10241) in the 1st Battalion, Honourable Artillery Company, when he died on 17 November 1918, six days after the end of the war, not from any wounds received in the heat of battle, but from the flu epidemic that had spread its tentacles of death across the world. He was 20 years of age and was the youngest of the six sons. On 11 August 1917 he had been given fourteen days leave to return to the UK, enabling him to spend some valuable time with his family. He returned to France after his furlough, but on 8 November, three days before the war's end, he was struck down with influenza. The sadness for his family of knowing that he had survived the war only to be so cruelly taken from them by the flu epidemic can only be guessed at. When he had enlisted on 10 June 1916 in Romford, he was a month shy of his eighteenth birthday. It would be another year before he arrived in France on 10 July 1917, but only four months later he would be dead.

Four of Frank and Charles's brothers also served their king and country in the armed forces during the First World War.

Edward Thomas **Bill** had been both a driver (208) and a bombardier (880152) in the Royal Field Artillery, having first arrived in France on 17 November 1915. He was awarded the 1915 Star, the British War Medal and the Victory Medal.

Arthur Michael **Bill**, like his brother Charles, also served as a private (426472) with the 3rd Battalion, Canadian Infantry, during the First World War and thankfully survived. It is quite possible that he was also involved in the heavy fighting at Mont Sorrel in Belgium.

Bernard William **Bill** was the oldest of the brothers, having been born in 1889. He passed away in 1977 in Surrey aged 88. We have not be able to confirm with any degree of certainty which regiments either Bernard or John Hubert Bill served with during the First World War.

CHAPTER 8

Rainham War Memorial

The Rainham War Memorial commemorates the names of those who died in both the First and Second World Wars, as well as the civilian casualties of the latter. The monument is a clock tower which can be found in the centre of the town. It cost a grand total of sixty pounds to build. It is constructed of red Belgian brick, with Portland stone dressings, and is somewhat unusual in that it is hexagonal in shape with clock faces on three of its sides. The names of the war dead are inscribed on the base of the memorial. In addition, it also incorporates stone blocks which have the inscription 'Lest We Forget' engraved. Iron railings surround the memorial, which is prominently sited between the Broadway and Upminster Road in front of the town's Saint Helen and Saint Giles churches.

The Rainham War Memorial was unveiled by Colonel Sir Francis Henry Douglas Charlton Whitmore on 7 November 1920. He'd had an interesting and varied military career and was as distinguished and noteworthy an individual as was possible to have attended the unveiling of

The Rainham War Memorial.
(Sean Connolly)

the memorial. He was originally commissioned into the 1st Essex Artillery Volunteers way back in 1892. He later transferred to the Essex Yeomanry before serving with the Imperial Yeomanry in the second Boer War (1899-1902). He was promoted to the rank of lieutenant colonel in 1915 and ended up commanding the 10th Royal Lancers during the First World War, during which he was mentioned in despatches on four occasions. He was awarded the Distinguished Service Order in 1917. He lived at Orsett near Grays. He had been a Justice of the Peace as far back as 1898, when only 26 years of age. He was High Sheriff of Essex in 1922 and Lord Lieutenant from 1936 to 1958. He died in 1962 aged 90 and was buried at Orsett parish church with full military honours.

One of those whose name is commemorated on the war memorial is that of second lieutenant Ralph Luxmore Curtis. During the war he was a pilot in the Royal Flying Corps and was credited with fifteen 'kills'. As a 19-year-old he had the distinction of engaging Hermann Göring in aerial combat. Göring finished the war with twenty-two claimed victories and during the Second World War would become the Commander in Chief of the Luftwaffe.

These are the names of the fifty-eight young men who are commemorated on the Rainham War Memorial:

P **Restell**	H **Davis**	G F **Blaxland**
J **Swann**	W J **Gregory**	S **Barnard**
F **Martin**	F **Burchell**	F **Sawkins**
J A **Whitby**	J **Harris**	W G **Jarvis**
W C **March**	G S **March**	E J **Holmes**
F **Hockley**	F G **Mansfield**	G E **Biggs**
E W **Butler**	A **Morant**	C **Morant**
J **Bones**	G T **Archer**	P **Letch**
R L **Curtis**	A **Lavender**	E **Smith**
E **Dunk**	E J **Stock**	F **Green**
S **Wiffen**	E T **Clayden**	E T **Sale**
W **Bishop**	F **Blighton**	W J E **Simmons**
H **Middleditch**	A G **Bullen**	J **Deeks**
H S **Burr**	E **Tunbridge**	E G **Keeble**
H **Manning**	H **Ireson**	W **Wood**
R **Beaumont**	E **Innell**	J **Biggs**

S **Bones**	R J **Chrisfield**	E J **Moore**
H S **Eady**	J **Strong**	R **Deeks**
E P **Aylwin**	H C **Martin**	J T **Wilson**
G S **Wilson**		

We have taken a look at some of these individuals in more detail.

George Stanley **Wilson** was a private (27871) in the 1st Battalion, Northamptonshire Regiment, when he was killed on 10 November 1917. His name is commemorated on the Arras War Memorial. The 1911 census shows the Wilson family living at number 8, Blewitt's Cottages, South Hornchurch. The parents were John and Mary Ann who, besides George, had two other sons, John, who was the oldest at 25 and Albert, who was 23. They also had a daughter, Nora, who at 13 was the youngest of their four children. George was seventeen at the time and was a labourer on one of the many surrounding farms.

John Thomas **Wilson** was a private (G/22997) in the 7th Battalion, the Queens (Royal West Surrey) Regiment, when he died on 3 September 1918, and only ten months after his brother George had been killed. He is buried at Barking's Rippleside Cemetery in Essex. In the circumstances we can only assume that John was wounded, returned to the United Kingdom to have his wounds treated, and died in hospital.

Albert Wilson was such a popular name during the late 1800s and early 1900s, it has not been possible for us to identify the Albert we were looking for, although it is inconceivable that he did not serve his king and country in its hour of need.

R.J. **Chrisfield** is one of the names engraved on the Rainham War Memorial. He was a sapper (358062) in the 1st Field Survey Company, Royal Engineers, when he died on 4 March 1919, according to the Commonwealth War Graves Commission website. Armed with the above information we then searched the 1911 census but could not find a direct match. The census showed that there were a lot of Chrisfields, most of whom were either born in or lived in the Kent area, but none with the initials R J, and none who came from the Rainham area of Essex. We then searched the Army Service Records on ancestry.co.uk. Once again we could find no direct match, but fortunately there were only three names listed, a Francis Chrisfield from South Norwood, a Philip Goodhew Chrisfield from Sheerness in Kent, and a James Richard Chrisfield from Battersea, who was the first name on the list.

Bingo, we had found the person we were looking for. He had served in the Royal Engineers and his service number was 358062, so it was definitely the same man. He had enlisted on 1 February 1916 at Battersea in London at the age of 18 and his home address was recorded as being 2 Devonshire Terrace, Melville Road, Battersea. His line of work was shown as being a reader's assistant and his father's name was William. It was easy to see the confusion surrounding his name. Armed with an address, we returned to the 1911 census and found a William and Elizabeth Chrisfield who lived at number 35, Lavender Road, Battersea. They had three sons, James who was 13 having been born in 1898, William Alfred, who was 16, and John, who was 22. The clincher that it was the person we were looking for was that James's occupation was shown as that of a reader's assistant. In his Army Service Record he was referred to as James Richard Christfield, Richard Christfield, R.J. Chrisfield and James Christfield, just to add to the confusion. The first ten months of his army life were spent in England training and preparing for war. He eventually departed via Southampton for the continent on 21 December 1916, arriving in France the next day. He was given a twenty-four-hour pass on the morning of Christmas day, having to be back in camp by 0630 hours the following morning, Boxing Day. Unfortunately for him he was late back from his furlough and so was punished by having one day's pay deducted from his wages. James married Elizabeth Mitchel, who was also 21 years of age, on 23 January 1918 at St Peter's Church in Battersea; the vicar who married them was George Bell. He was admitted to the Stationary Hospital in Paris on 4 February 1919 complaining of a pain in his side. His condition worsened and he passed away at seven o'clock in the morning on 4 March 1919. The telegram which was sent to his wife Elizabeth informing her of her husband's death referred to him as James Richard Chrisfield. He was buried in the City of Paris Cemetery in Pantin, France.

This is the first time I have heard mention of this cemetery during the research for this book. The earliest burials which took place there were in late 1914 and were of Allied soldiers who had died of their wounds in the city's hospitals. It wasn't really used again for military burials until the summer of 1918, when it was used for British troops who were fighting the Germans in the nearby areas of the Aisne and

Marne. There are also a number of burials in the cemetery of British and Commonwealth troops who died after the armistice. There are nearly 100 burials in the cemetery of British, Commonwealth and Allied combatants who were killed in the fighting of the First World War or who died of their wounds.

James Chrisfield's brother William had also served during the war, in the Royal Navy. He survived the war and eventually died in Lambeth on 7 November 1958.

I could find no record of John Thomas Chrisfield, either having served in the armed forces or having been one of its casualties.

F.G. **Blighton** was a private (267311) in the 2nd/5th Battalion, Gloucestershire Regiment, when he was killed in action aged 22 on 21 March 1918. The British Army's First World War medal rolls index cards show a private (267311) Frederick G. Blighton who had previously served in the Essex Regiment as Private 2705 and who had also had the service number of 6089 while in the Gloucestershire Regiment. The 1911 census shows that Mr and Mrs Edward and Emma Blighton lived at number 34, Normandy Terrace, Cowper Road, Rainham, Essex, with their four sons, Frederick, who was 15, Sidney, 13, and Percy and Edward, who were 4 and 2. They also had three daughters, Eleanor, who was 12, Winifred, who was 10, and Kate, who was the youngest of the girls at 8. I could find no record of Sidney having served in the military during the First World War. By the early 1920s Frederick's parents, along with their three youngest children, had moved to number 2, Tennyson Cottages, Cowper Road, Rainham. Frederick is buried in the picturesque and peaceful surroundings of the Villers-Bretonneux Military Cemetery in the Somme region of France.

Villers-Bretonneux Military Cemetery. (**Commonwealth War Graves Commission**)

It is not only an idyllic location, but tender loving care has obviously gone into its maintenance as well.

The village of Villers-Bretonneux was captured by the Germans on 23 April 1918 while on their way to Amiens, using their tanks and infantry. The village was recaptured the very next day by Australian forces. The cemetery is unusual in that it wasn't even begun until 1920, when the bodies of Commonwealth soldiers who had originally been buried in cemeteries in the surrounding areas were brought to the cemetery to be laid to rest for the final time. This work wasn't completed until 1925 by which time the number of graves had reached 2,142. The cemetery also contains the Australian National War Memorial which commemorates the names of 10,765 Australian soldiers who fought and died throughout France and Belgium during the First World War. It was unveiled by King George Vl on 22 July 1938.

G.F. **Blaxland** was George Frederick **Blaxland**, a stoker 1st class (SS/113116) in the Royal Navy, who was serving on the Royal Naval Battleship HMS *Formidable* on 1 January 1915 when she was sunk by two torpedoes that had been fired by the German submarine *U-24*. His name is commemorated on the Chatham Naval Memorial.

George was one of the 547 officers and men who were killed, from a ship's complement of 780.

HMS *Formidable* was commissioned in 1904 and before the First World War she was part of both the Mediterranean and Channel fleets. When war broke out in 1914 she was part of the 5th Battle Squadron who were stationed at Sheerness on the Isle of Sheppey. Her remit was to conduct operations in the English Channel because of the real concerns that Germany intended to invade Great Britain. On 30 December 1914 the 5th Battle Squadron were replaced by the 6th Battle Squadron and transferred to Portland on the south coast. With a war on there was no time to let

HMS Formidable.
(Wikipedia)

things come to a standstill so that military personnel could take time off and celebrate New Year's Eve; that simply wasn't practicable. HMS *Formidable* and her crew were participating in gunnery exercises off the Isle of Portland and once the exercises had finished they remained at sea on patrol even though German submarine activity had been reported in the English Channel. Because of the inclement weather of rough seas, rain and high winds, the prospect of a possible submarine attack wasn't treated as a significant threat. New Year's Day 1915 was only two hours and twenty minutes old when the first of *U-24*'s torpedoes struck HMS *Formidable*. Within the space of twenty minutes she was already listing by some twenty degrees to starboard. Realizing there was no chance of saving his ship, and with a strong desire to save as many of his men as possible, Captain Noel Loxley gave the order to abandon ship. Because of the worsening weather conditions and the darkness, getting the rest of the men who had survived the attack off the boat safely was never going to be easy. This wasn't helped any when the ship was struck by a second torpedo just after three o'clock. Less than two hours later, at a quarter to five, she capsized and sank beneath the waves.

James **Deeks** was born in 1898 in Rainham. When he enlisted he became a private (119790) in the 29th Battalion Machine Gun Corps (Infantry). He was killed on 12 April 1918. He was awarded the British War Medal and the Victory Medal and his name is commemorated on the Ploegsteert War Memorial in the Hainault area of Belgium. The memorial commemorates the names of some 11,000 South African and British servicemen who fell during fighting in the area and who have no known grave.

Percy James Draper **Restell** was a private (10078) in the 1st Battalion, Queens Own (Royal West Kent) Regiment. Born in Grays in 1894, he enlisted on 28 January 1913 at Maidstone, prior to which he had been a railway porter. He died of his wounds on 7 November 1914 and is buried at the Boulogne Eastern Cemetery in the Pas-de-Calais. Boulogne was one of three most extensively used ports by Commonwealth forces on the Western Front during the First World War. It was also one of the region's chief hospital locations. Percy spent the first seventeen months of his military service in England before arriving in France as part of the British Expeditionary Force on 14

August 1914 and less than three months later he was dead, dying on 7 November 1914 from wounds he received in action. In response to two letters which he had written to the War Office requesting his late son's medals be sent to him, a typed letter was sent in reply to Percy's father, Mr J. Restell of 98 Upper Stone Street, Maidstone, from the Infantry Records Office, Hounslow, dated 27 September 1921:

> *Sir,*
>
> *With reference to your letter dated 20 September 1921, I am directed to inform you that under instructions from the War Office, all medals awarded to your son above named, are the legal property of Miss Lily O'Neill, of 43 North Brunswick Street, Dublin, to whom the decorations have been despatched.*
>
> *Yours faithfully,*
>
> *Captain for Colonel,*
>
> *In charge Infantry Records Office*

Ten months later a similar letter was sent to Percy's sister, Mrs S. Davey of 44 Charles Street, Grays, Essex, after she too had requested the same medals be forwarded on to her. It is not clear whether she knew of the previous attempt by her father to acquire the medals. Reading through Percy's Army Service Record it becomes apparent that Lilly O'Neil was his wife, who we are assuming had reverted back to her maiden name and title on his untimely death. On 4 September 1915 Lilly received a package which contained the personal belongings of her dear departed husband, Percy. This included a holdall, a pipe, letters and other correspondence, a belt, two razors, a brush and some soap. Reading through the letters which both Percy's father and sister wrote to the War Office, requesting his medals, it is not clear whether they knew of Percy's marriage to Lilly. Two possibilities immediately come to mind, firstly that they did know of the marriage and that there was disharmony between them and Percy's wife, or secondly, Percy had not told his family about his marriage to Lilly. The matter was not made any clearer when Lilly sent the following letter to the Infantry Record Office, dated 16 June 1919:

> *Sir,*

This morning I received a form to fill up about the relatives of the late 10078 Private PJD Restell RWK. As I cannot give you any information of any one belong[ing] to him, I should be very thankful if you should let me know what I should do about the form.

I remain sir, your humble servant,

L. O Neil

If Lilly genuinely didn't know any information about his family and their whereabouts, the obvious question is why? To further add to the confusion, on 29 December 1919, the Infantry Records Office in Hounslow wrote to Percy's father requesting he fill out an 'Army Form W.5080', which they had enclosed. In essence, this was a statement requesting all of the names and addresses of all of Percy's living relatives. In the box next to 'Widow of the Soldier', which was for her name in full, the word 'single' has been written, which is somewhat strange as they already knew that when Percy died on 1 November 1914, some five years earlier, he was already married to Lilly. The form also showed that Percy had two brothers, James who was 13 and William, who was 11. He also had two sisters, Rosalind who was 17, and Rachel, who was 15. His mother was shown as being dead. The other interesting fact was that neither of the sisters' names began with the letter S. The letter and form had been sent out in relation to the Memorial Scroll and Medal which were sent to the next of kin of all soldiers who had died as a result of their wartime service. Even though Percy's medals, the 1914 Star, the British War Medal and the Victory Medal, had been sent to his wife Lilly, the Memorial Scroll and Medal were sent to Percy's father. In both the 1901 census, when he was only 7 years of age, and the 1911 census, when he was 17, he was living with his grandparents, William and Fanny Musgrove of number 97, High Street, Grays. Why he was not living with his mother and father is not explained. As interesting as all of this is, we could not find any direct or obvious link connecting Percy with the town of Rainham.

The Rainham Church of St Helen & St Giles has a roll of honour on a marble plaque on one of the pillars within the church. It has fifty names engraved on it, commemorating those from the parish who fell during the First World War. Every one of the names is also recorded on the main Rainham War Memorial.

Roll of Honour – St Helen & St Giles Church. (Sean Connolly)

CHAPTER 9

St Mary & St Peter's Church Wennington – Roll of Honour

Wennington Roll of Honour. (Sean Connolly)

The Wennington Roll of Honour for those men who lost their lives during the First World War can be found in the town's St Mary & St Peter's Church. There are only ten names on the plaque which bears their names, but each and every one of them were remembered fondly and with pride by the friends and family who they left behind. They went off to fight for their king and country with gusto and vigour, each of them paying the ultimate price so that those they left behind could have a better and safer tomorrow.

Ager, A	**Ashwell**, A J	**Baker**, J
Cansdale, C	**Carter**, W	**Challis**, J
Cox, E	**Morgan**, A	**Phillips**, G
Ward, G		

We will take a closer look at a few of these names:

Charles **Cansdale** was a private (2226) in the 1st Battalion, Essex Regiment. He was born in Bures in Suffolk and enlisted at Warley on the outskirts of Brentwood. Charles and his comrades from the 1st Battalion, Essex Regiment, arrived at Cape Helles on the Gallipoli Peninsular on 25 April 1915 and were almost immediately involved in heavy fighting with their Turkish foes. Less than a month later Charles would be dead. He died of his wounds sustained in the fighting on 21 May 1915 and was buried at the Alexandria (Chatby) Military and War Memorial Cemetery, which was originally called the Garrison Cemetery, in Egypt.

The cemetery was used for burials from the beginning of the fighting up until April 1916, although the remains of others who had died and been buried elsewhere were brought to the cemetery after the war had ended. There are a total of 2,259 Commonwealth servicemen buried in the cemetery. Contained within the cemetery is the Chatby War Memorial which commemorates the names of 1,000 Commonwealth servicemen who were killed or died during the First World War and whose bodies were sadly never recovered. The principal reason for this was that they were lost at sea when the hospital or transport ships they were being carried on were sunk by the either the German navy or the Luftwaffe while sailing to or from the Port of Alexandria.

Charles Cansdale had five brothers, four of whom were old enough to have served in the First World War: Willie, who would have been 28 at the outbreak of war, Walter, who would have been 23, James, who would have been 22, and Arthur, who would have been 15. We have not been able to positively confirm whether any of them actually served in the war, although because of their ages it is difficult to believe that they didn't. The fifth brother, Bertie, would have only been 8 years of age at the start of the war.

There is an interesting aside to this story in that there were two other men with the name Charles Cansdale who were born in Bures and died during the First World War. One of them was Charles James Cansdale, who was a 19-year-old private (18715) serving in the 11th Battalion, Essex Regiment, and who was killed on 13 June 1916 during fighting on the Western Front. The other one was Charles John Cansdale, who was a 36-year-old private (46380) serving with the Royal Army Medical Corps. He died of his wounds on 14 March 1916.

Arthur John **Ashwell** was a private (3273) (200961) in the 4th Battalion, Essex Regiment, which was a Territorial unit made up of men mainly, but not exclusively, from the Romford area.

He was born at Henlow, Bedfordshire, in 1895, and at the time of his death he was 22 years of age. According to the 1911 census he was a farm labourer, which was a common line of work for young men of his age. His parents, Harry and Clara, lived at number 5, New Cottages, Wennington, near Rainham. He had an elder brother, Archibald, who was 19, and a younger sister, Elsie Maude, who was 11.

Like his brother, Archibald had been a farm labourer before the war; but the similarities didn't stop there, as Archibald was also a private (2288) (200537) in the 4th Battalion, Essex Regiment, having enlisted some six weeks after the outbreak of war on 29 September 1914 when he was 22 years of age. Whether Archibald and Arthur enlisted on the same day is not known, but if they did they certainly did not do so together, as Archibald enlisted at Brentwood, while Arthur enlisted in Ilford. It would be ten months before Archibald left to serve abroad, arriving in the Balkans peninsular on 21 July 1915. One month later, on 31 August 1915, he was wounded in action, although there is no mention of what his injuries were. It can only be assumed that whatever they were they weren't fatal, as in another two months he would return home to England. In November 1916, while still in England, Archibald was disciplined for being absent without leave, an offence for which he was punished by having to forfeit five day's pay. If he had committed the same offence while serving abroad, there is every possibility he would have faced a court martial, and if found guilty could have faced a firing squad for desertion. On 5 May 1917

Archibald was transferred to Class 'P' Territorial Reserve and seven months later, on 21 December 1917, he was discharged from the army for 'being no longer physically fit for war service – Para. 392 (xvi) K.R.' Although there was no explanation on his service record as to what the specific ailment was which had rendered him so medically unfit for war service, the following paragraph had been added:

Permanently excluded from liability to medical re-examination under the Military Service (Review of Exemptions) Act 1917.

Underneath this was a section with the heading 'Character'. Intriguingly enough it said, 'Not yet assessed', which seems somewhat of a strange statement as by the time of his medical discharge he had been in the army for three years. Archibald lived to the ripe old age of 89 before passing away in March 1981 at Epping.

Sadly Arthur's Army Service Record has not survived so we have not been able to provide as much information about him. We do know that he was killed in action on 27 March 1917 while serving in Palestine, which at the time was part of the greater Turkish Empire. His name is commemorated on the Jerusalem War Memorial in Israel.

Both brothers were awarded the British War Medal and the Victory Medal, with Archibald additionally receiving the 1915 Star.

Jack **Challis** was born in 1897 in Romford to James and Mary Challis. At the time of the 1911 census the family were living at number 12, New Cottages, Wennington, Essex. Jack became a gunner (L/1544) in the 83rd Battery, 11th Brigade, Royal Field Artillery, but sadly was killed soon after his nineteenth birthday on 7 August 1916 and is buried at the Albert Communal Cemetery Extension, Somme, France.

The extension section of the cemetery was first used by units of the British Army and Field Ambulance in August 1915 and continued to be used all the way through until November 1916 by other units such as the 5th Casualty Clearing station. There are a total of 862 Commonwealth graves from the First World War in the cemetery.

Jack had an elder brother, George William Challis, who was born in 1893. He also served during the First World War. He was attested on 19 November 1915 at Grays, but it would be nearly another year before he was mobilized on 7 November 1916 at Warley Barracks on the outskirts of Brentwood. Like his brother Jack, George became a gunner

(194393) in the 7th Reserve Brigade, Royal Field Artillery. He was admitted to Cambridge General Hospital on 18 August 1917 for a total of seventy-three days for impetigo, a skin complaint which can leave a patient in much discomfort and which can be acutely debilitating. He was finally released to return to his unit on 30 October 1917. On 14 June 1918, when in barracks at Felixstowe, he was caught by his lieutenant and corporal gambling in his hut. He went before a discipline board, was found guilty, and confined to barracks for seven days. In the circumstances, I'm not totally sure that this punishment would have prevented the offence he had committed from occurring again. On 4 December 1918 he was transferred to the Royal Army Service Corps where he became a private (R/447294) at their depot in Ormskirk, which is a market town in West Lancashire, fourteen miles north of Liverpool city centre.

He was finally demobbed on 23 October 1919 at Woolwich Dockyard in London. The family home, where he still lived with his parents, had now moved and was at number 1, Ashley Terrace, Melville Road, Rainham.

G. **Phillips** was a private (201037) in the 1st/4th Battalion, Essex Regiment, when he was killed on 26 March 1917 aged 22. A native of Wennington, he is buried at the Gaza War Cemetery. At the end of March 1917, Gaza was in the hands of Turkish Forces who were being attacked and surrounded by the battalions of the Egyptian Expeditionary Force, of which Private Phillips and his Essex comrades were a part. The allied attack was stopped when the Turkish defenders were suddenly bolstered by reinforcements. It was during this sustained period of fighting that Private Phillips became yet another of the war's casualties. The Gaza War Cemetery contains the graves of 3,217 Commonwealth servicemen from the First World War; 781 of these remain unidentified. Private Phillips's parents, James and Emma, lived at number 4, Bentham Square, Blue Town, Sheerness, Kent.

CHAPTER 10

Hornchurch War Memorial

The Hornchurch War Memorial stands proudly outside St Andrew's Church in the High Street, for all to see and remember the price those named on it paid for the greater good of mankind. The inscription on the war memorial reads as follows:

The Great War 1914-1919

These, at the call of King and country, left all that was dear to them, endured hardness, faced danger and finally passed out of the sight of men by the path of duty and self-sacrifice; giving up their own lives that others may live in freedom.

(Photograph by Stuart Lynch)

Let those who come after see their names are not forgotten.

They were a wall unto us by both night and by day.

The names which are commemorated on the memorial are as follows:

Abraham W	**Adams** S	**Allcock** W
Alexander W W	**Aley** F R	**Aley** S A
Archer F	**Axup** V E	**Aylwin** E P
Bacon A F	**Baker** C H	**Barber** W
Barker F	**Barnes** S K	**Barrington** L S
Beard C J	**Beer** L A	**Bennett** E A
Bill C S	**Bill** F K	**Bishop** J D

Blackwell L B	**Bradley** R J	**Bridge** W S
Brockhurst J	**Brown** E D	**Bull** F H
Burgess F	**Button** C H	**Cantle** F S
Card J V	**Cardy** G	**Chester** F G
Chinnery G	**Clark** H L	**Bristow** S R
Clyde H	**Coe** F W	**Cole** H
Collin F W	**Collister** W	**Cook** H
Cooper H	**Cox** G W	**Creek** A C
Cressey G J	**Cressey** J F	**Cressey** W J
Crow R J	**Curtis** C	**Curtis** R
Daeth W S	**Daniels** E J	**Dawson** R J
Day A C	**Dean** A	**Digby** A V
Dix H C	**Doe** F S	**Dorling** F
Downham E	**Dunlop** E A	**Dunlop** P A
Eaton H	**Ellis** A	**Fardell** S E
Farrant A R	**Farrant** H R	**Field** S D
Finch R T	**Fitzjohn** W	**Flack** J
Fletcher C	**Ford** A	**Ford** H
Forest E	**Fox** W R S	**Franklyn** G W
Frost C W	**Frost** T G	**Frost** W G
Fry B R	**Garrett** E A	**Gaywood** J E
Gibson A	**Goodwin** R R	**Goodwin** E H
Gray A	**Green** E	**Grimwood** F
Grottick P C	**Grout** H	**Grout** L A J
Guy W F	**Guymer** S J	**Hammond** J D
Hammond W G	**Hanson** A	**Harvey** L H
Hawkins J R	**Hayward** P	**Haywood** W A
Healing H F	**Hills** A T	**Hills** H G
Hitch H P	**Hobbs** N	**Horsnell** J
Howell R	**Hunwicks** J	**Hutchinson** L
Jarvis A	**Kemp** G H	**Kendall** F D
King A E	**King** C T	**Knight** A C
Knight G H	**Knight** H C	**Lazell** A F
Leech T	**Letten** T	**Little** C W
Little J	**Livermore** P	**Long** B W
Long J J	**Love** J	**Lungley** J A
Macey C J	**Maidment** G	**Mason** J

Matthews F L	**Millard** J	**Miller** P
Page R	**Parsons** A	**Pailthorpe** H A
Nicholls E W	**Parker** H	**Pearce** A
Pewter B J	**Peto** A	**Poole** A H
Moss H P	**Powell** L A	**Prior** B S
Purkis F W	**Purkis** W E	**Marrable** T
Marrable J	**Marshall** W J	**Martin** H C
Martin W A	**Mayes** W	**Mayne** T
Ramsay	**Rolfe** F	**Saggers** F
Saunders G	**Saunders** H	**Searle** H E
Shearman J	**Shelley** G	**Shield** W
Sibthorp J J	**Simpson** J	**Skingley** H W
Sledge W	**Smith** A	**Smith** P
Smith S	**South** A E	**Stebbings** S
Tattersall F	**Taylor** H A	**Taylor** W A
Thorogood H W	**Tickner** W J	**Trotman** H T
Tucker H E	**Turner** E S	**Turvey** F L J
Tyler R	**Utley** F C	**Vale** A
Veale A A	**Viney** C W	**Wakeling** G
Wall F J	**Wallis** E	**Ward** J
Wardill G E	**Warman** W R	**Warren** A S
Webb A S	**Webb** F	**Webb** P E
Whipps A	**Whipps** W V	**Whitams** T R
White G F	**White** J W G	**Wilson** E
Wilson G S	**Wilson** J T	**Wright** E
York W J	**Young** H A	**Pwepper** J
Moss T	**Nichols** E W	

Leslie Stuart **Barrington** was a private (13774) in the 7th Battalion, Lincolnshire Regiment, when he was killed in action on the Western Front on 20 December 1915, just as the second Christmas of the war was approaching. He had only been in France for five months before he was killed, arriving there on 14 July. His name is commemorated on the Menin Road North Memorial which is located at the Menin Road South Military Cemetery.

The cemetery was first used by the 8th Battalion, South Staffordshire Regiment, and the 9th Battalion, East Surrey Regiment, in January

1916. It continued to be used for Allied and Commonwealth burials up until the summer months of 1918. After the war had ended, the remains of soldiers who had been buried in nearby ad hoc locations were brought to the cemetery for reburial.

The 1911 census shows that Leslie Stuart Barrington was born in Southgate in Hertfordshire in 1896, but that he was living at number 8, Vincent Road, Highams Park, Walthamstow. It must have been somewhat of a big house as he lived there with his seven brothers and sisters. His elder brother Ralph, who was 28 and a commercial clerk for a firm of civil mining engineers, was the head of the household. The 1901 census shows their father as Frederick G. Barrington, who at 48 years of age was still a relatively young man. As there is no sign of him on the 1911 census, we can only assume that he died sometime in between the two dates.

One of Leslie's brothers, Roland, who was a year older than him, had also joined the 7th Battalion, Lincolnshire Regiment, having enlisted at Walthamstow on 5 September 1914. In an awful twist of fate, Leslie and Roland were both killed in action on the very same day, possibly even in the same action. In death they were reunited with each other when they were placed next to each other in the same cemetery. We could find no obvious connection between Leslie and Hornchurch or a suitable explanation as to why Roland's name isn't commemorated on the same memorial.

Frederick Sipthorp **Cantle** was a private (2572) in the 8th Battalion, The Queens (Royal West Surrey) Regiment. He was 25 years of age when he died of his wounds on 25 May 1916. He is buried at the Bailleul Communal Cemetery Extension, in the Nord region of France. He enlisted at St Paul's Churchyard in London, one would assume because that's near to where he was working at the time as a clerk in the building trade. The 1911 census shows the Cantle family of Henry and Annie-Marie and their two children, Ethel and Frederick, living at 'Burslem', Parkstone Avenue, Emerson Park, Hornchurch. After the war Frederick's father Henry, who was by now a widower, had moved and was living at a property named 'Temple', in Corsley, Warminster, Wiltshire.

Archie Raymond **Farrant** and Hector Reginald **Farrant** were brothers. Hector, the youngest, was the first to die, less than two weeks after the First World War had officially ended, on 24 November 1918. He was only just 18 years of age and an air mechanic 3rd class in the Royal Air Force stationed at the Receiving Depot in Blandford, Dorset. There has been a military camp there since 1724, which over the years has been home to the Royal Air Force, the Royal Navy, the United States Army and the British Army.

Archie was a corporal in the Essex Regiment (1726) before transferring to the 4th Battalion, Duke of Cambridge's Own (Middlesex) Regiment, still with the rank of a corporal (34102). He was 23 years of age when he died on 15 November 1919; nearly a year after Hector had passed away. Both Archie and Hector are buried in the same grave at St Andrew's Churchyard in their home town of Hornchurch, sharing the same headstone.

Archie and Hector Farrant's headstone. (Sean Connolly)

The Church has a total of thirty-seven service men who died as a result of their involvement in the First World War buried in its grounds.

With both brothers having died after the war had finished and in the absence of their Military Service Records having survived, and with the added factor of them both being buried at St Andrew's Churchyard in Hornchurch, we are going to assume the possibility that they both went to their graves having fallen victim to the influenza pandemic that was sweeping across the world at the time. The 1911 census shows the family was living at number 25, Cyril Villas, Douglas Road, Romford. There was another brother, Frederick G., who at 17 was the eldest of William and Mary Farrant's four children. At only 4 years of age, sister Winnie was the baby of the family. We could find no record of Frederick having served in the First World War. The only references we could find for a Frederick Farrant who had been born in 1894 was one who had by 1915 moved to the United States. The 1901 census showed that William and Mary Farrant had three other children, William H., who was then 13 years of age, Eleanor M.A., who was 11, and Evelyn, who was 9. Both of the girls went into domestic service, Eleanor with the Penney family in Great Warley and Evelyn with the Moore family in Romford.

Walter Charles **Fitzjohn** was born in Brentwood in 1884, lived in Hornchurch, and had enlisted at nearby Romford. He was 33 years of age and a private (19226) in the 2nd Battalion, Essex Regiment, when he was killed in action on 3 May 1917. His name is commemorated on the Arras War Memorial in the Pas-de-Calais. The memorial commemorates the names of some 35,000 officers and men from both South African and Commonwealth forces who were killed in the Arras area between March 1916 and 7 August 1918, which was the eve of the final Allied push to victory. During April and May 1917, a period in time that history has recorded as the Arras Offensive, Walter was killed fighting with his friends and colleagues. The Essex regiment lost a total of 109 officers and men on 3 May 1917. All of those who are commemorated on the Arras War Memorial have no known grave. Before the war he and his wife Emma, lived at Herongate on the outskirts of Brentwood. They had a 5-year-old daughter, also named Emma. After the war mum and daughter, now without a husband and father, moved to Wells Cottage, Ardleigh Green, in nearby Hornchurch.

Arras War Memorial. **(Commonwealth War Graves Commission)**

Percy Charles **Grottick** was a sergeant (31556) in the 8th Battalion, Royal Welsh Fusiliers. The Regiment was formed in August 1914 in Wrexham in Wales and came under orders of the 40th Brigade of the 13th Western Division of the British Army who, in July 1915, sailed for Mudros, a port on the Mediterranean island of Lemnos. For Percy this was only three months after having recovered from a broken leg, an injury which saw him spend nearly two months recovering in hospital in Aldershot. Percy had enlisted very early in the war, on 19 August 1914. He was promoted to the rank of corporal on 1 December 1915 and, just twenty-eight days later on 29 December, he was further promoted to the rank of sergeant. The speed of the latter promotion probably came about as a result of the deaths of sergeants in his company and battalion. He was killed in action on 9 April 1916, possibly in fighting against Turkish forces while trying to relieve the garrison at Kut al Amara. His name is commemorated on the Basra War Memorial in Iraq which includes the names of some 45,000 officers and servicemen from Commonwealth forces who died in what was then Mesopotamia and today covers the countries of Kuwait, Iraq and parts of Syria, Turkey and Iran. Percy's death was particularly sad for his father, George Henry, who lived at 'Kilimacolin', Squirrels Heath, Romford. He was a widower and Percy was his only son.

George **Maidment** was a family man who worked in the General Post Office in London as a sorter in the Foreign Section. By the time the First World War had begun in 1914, he had been married to his wife Alice for seventeen years, marrying in London on 22 August 1896. They had four children, two sons, and two daughters. Arthur was the eldest, born just a year after George and Alice had married. Ellen came along next, a few years later followed by May and Percival who were twins. They also had a nephew, Sidney Maidment, aged 7, living with them as well. According to the 1911 census, the family lived at a property called 'Fernlea' in Ernest Road in Hornchurch, although for many years they must have lived in Clapham, South London, as that is where all four of the children were born. When the war started, George enlisted at his local recruitment office in Romford although, being 42 years of age and a married man with kids, there was at that time no requirement for him to do so. He joined the 18th Service Battalion, Kings Royal Rifle Corps, where he eventually became a corporal

(C/6544). As a younger man, and well before the First World War had even been thought of, he had previously served with the 4th Battalion, Middlesex Regiment. He was killed on 13 November 1916, less than two months after he had transferred from the 18th Battalion to the 1st Battalion and, although his body was never recovered from the field of battle, his name is commemorated for evermore on the Thiepval War Memorial on the Somme. A very brave man who like so many of his comrades paid the ultimate price in serving his king and country to the detriment of himself and his family.

John Henry **Horsnell** was born in Grays in 1884 and the 1901 census shows him living at number 7, Darnley Road, Grays, with his parents, Thomas and Mary, and his two brothers, William, who was 11, and Harry, who was 3. John's occupation was recorded as being a stonemason's apprentice. Although William and Harry were both old enough to have served during the First World War, we can find no record of them having done so. We do know that Harry died in 1956 at the relatively young age of 58. At the beginning of the First World War he was a police constable with the local Essex Constabulary, stationed at Romford Police station. He lived with his wife Edith, who was six years older than him, at number 34 Malvern Road, Romford. When he decided that he wanted to enlist in the army, he did so at his local recruiting office in Romford and became a gunner (185387) with the 1st/1st Highland Brigade, Royal Garrison Artillery. He was killed on 25 March 1918 and is buried in the Anzin-St Aubin British Cemetery in the Pas-de-Calais.

Anzin-St Aubin British Cemetery. **(Commonwealth War Graves Commission)**

The cemetery contains 358 burials of British or Commonwealth servicemen who fell during the First World War, 145 of whom were soldiers specifically from artillery units.

The 1911 census showed the **Pailthorpe** family living at 'Fairmead' in Carter Road, Hornchurch. Henry and Caroline Pailthorpe had five children, four sons and a daughter. Harold was the eldest at 20 and after leaving school went to work as a clerk to a firm of stockbrokers in London. He qualified as a pilot flying a Graham-White biplane at the Royal Naval Air Station at Chingford on 11 May 1916 and became a flight lieutenant in the Royal Naval Air Service. He was killed in action on 23 May 1917 while serving in France and is buried in the Cabaret-Rouge British Cemetery at Souchez in the Pas-de-Calais, which also happens to be the final resting place of another seventy officers from either the Royal Flying Corps, the Royal Naval Air Service or the Royal Air Force.

Cabaret-Rouge British Cemetery.
(Commonwealth War Graves Commission)

One of Harold's brothers, Edward, also served during the war as a private (38935) in the Royal Army Medical Corps. According to the 1911 census, Harold was only 13 years of age. It is quite conceivable that he turned 14 sometime later that year, but he must have just turned 18 when he enlisted as he arrived in France on 29 September 1915. He was awarded the 1915 Star, the British War Medal and the Victory Medal for his wartime service. Unlike the unfortunate Harold, Edward survived the war, finally passing away on 18 June 1964 aged 66. He left the sizeable sum of £4,368 in his will.

In 1911 the **Marrable** family lived at 'Thatched House', Lower Road in Cranham, and even though Thomas Marrable was a comparatively young man at only 48, he was already a widower. He was left with five children to bring up all on his own. Two sons and three daughters. His eldest son, also named Thomas, was 15-year-old baker's assistant in 1911. Thomas would go on to enlist in the army and become a rifleman (R/14075) in the 8th Battalion, Kings Royal Rifle Corps. He was killed in action on 3 September 1916 aged 21. His name is commemorated on the Thiepval War Memorial in the Somme.

The overriding battle at the time of Thomas's death was the Battle of the Somme which in effect was a series of smaller battles. There were three battles being fought on 3 September 1916. Delville Wood took place between 15 July and 3 September 1916, the Battle of Pozières took place between 23 July and 3 September 1916, and the Battle of Guillemont took place between 3 and 6 September 1916. Thomas's battalion were part of the 14th Light Division who fought at the Battle of Delville Wood, so it would appear that Thomas was killed on the very last day of the battle.

According to the 1911 census, Frederick Walter **Purkis** was born on 29 June 1892 in Romford. He lived at Hay Green in Hornchurch with his parents, John and Nellie, and his four younger brothers, Arthur, William, Charles and Albert. When it came time to do his bit for king and country, Frederick decided on joining the navy, where he became a stoker 1st class (K/19579). He survived the war but died on 20 January 1921 while on board HM Submarine *K5*. Interestingly enough, on his military record under the heading 'cause of death' it says, 'Killed or died by means other than disease, accident or enemy action.' That statement doesn't leave too much room for any other way to die. The facts of the matter are that the submarine he was on was taking part in Fleet exercises in the Atlantic Ocean when it suddenly and inexplicably disappeared off the Scilly Isles. All fifty-seven members of the crew on board at the time, including Frederick, were killed. He was awarded the 1914 Star, the British War Medal and the Victory Medal for his wartime efforts. By the time of his death, Frederick was married to Gladys and they lived at Hill Farm Cottage, Hacton Lane, Hornchurch.

Frederick's brother, William Ernest **Purkis**, also fell during the war. He started out as private 2383 in the 4th Battalion, Essex Regiment, which was a Territorial unit, but on promotion to the rank of corporal, his service number changed to 200579. Most of the men who served in the 4th Battalion came from the Hornchurch area, making it nearly, but not quite, a pals battalion. William was killed in action on 1 May 1918 in Palestine; he was 23 years of age. His name is commemorated at the Jerusalem Memorial in Israel. The Jerusalem War Memorial commemorates the names of some 3,300 servicemen from Commonwealth forces who died during the First World War while engaged in operations in Egypt and Palestine, and who have no known grave. Besides the 1915 Star, the British War Medal and the Victory Medal, he was also awarded the Military Medal for bravery in the face of the enemy.

During the First World War there were over 115,000 Military Medals awarded for acts of bravery. There were 5,700 men who went on to win a second Military Medal and even 180 men who were awarded the medal on a third occasion. One man, Private Ernest Albert Corey, who was a stretcher bearer in the 55th Australian Infantry Battalion, was awarded the medal a

Military Medal. **(Wikipedia)**

fourth time. The award of the medal was discontinued in 1993 and since then the Military Cross, which had previously only been awarded to officers, is now awarded to officers and men of all ranks.

The 1911 census shows that Frank Charles **Utley** lived with his parents, Charles and Kate, at number 49 Douglas Road, Romford, along with his elder brother Walter and his two younger sisters, Dorothy and Daphne Frank enlisted early on in the war at Handel Street in London. He joined the 1st (City of London) Battalion (Royal Fusiliers), where he eventually became a lance corporal (2295). He died of his wounds on 19 October 1915 after having been injured during fighting on the Western Front and returned to hospital in England. He is buried in St Andrew's Churchyard at Hornchurch. Despite Charles being 26 years of age at the start of the war in 1914, we could find no record of him having served in the British armed forces.

Mrs Emily Ellen Tattersall lived at number 8 George Street, Romford, with her two daughters, Maud and Muriel, and her 19-year-old son Frank, who was a railway clerk at Romford railway station. Emily's husband, Alfred Tattersall, was a Yorkshire man born in Wakefield in 1865, by trade a draper's assistant. For some reason the Tattersalls do not appear on the 1901 census, by which time all three children had already been born. On the 1911 census the family re-appear, but Alfred Tattersall is no longer shown as being part of the family. Instead, against Emily's marital status is the word 'Deserted'. For some reason, which is not recorded, Albert has left Emily to bring up their three children all on her own. Frank Alfred **Tattersall** enlisted within a month of the outbreak of war, signing up in September 1914, eventually becoming a sergeant (2579) in the 1st/6th Battalion, London Regiment (City of London Rifles). He was killed in action on 15 September 1916 aged 24. His name is commemorated on the Thiepval War Memorial in the Somme.

CHAPTER 11

St Thomas's Church Noak Hill - Roll of Honour

To The GLORY OF GOD
AND IN MEMORY OF THOSE MEN OF
NOAK HILL, WHO FELL IN THE GREAT WAR
1914–1919, FOR THE RIGHTS OF NATIONS
AND THE PEACE OF THE WORLD.

NAME	RANK	REGT.	DATE OF DEATH
COWLAND, W.	GUNNER,	R.H.A.	17. SEPT. 1917.
ELLINGWORTH, A.W.	GUNNER,	R.G.A.	5. MAY 1918.
LAUNDY, D.J.	LCE. CPL.	K.R.R.	24. AUG. 1917.
LAUNDY, E.W.	PRIVATE,	4TH ESSEX.	23. AUG. 1915.
NEAVE, A.	MAJOR,	16TH LANCERS.	21. FEB. 1915.
OVALL, T.	PRIVATE,	E. SURREY.	1. OCT. 1918.
STOKES, F.	PRIVATE,	10TH ESSEX.	19. JUNE 1918.
WRIGHT, C.C.	PRIVATE,	28TH OX. BUCKS.	22. AUG. 1917.
YETTON, C.V.	PRIVATE,	2ND LT. SCOTTISH.	30. APRIL 1918.

ERECTED BY THE PARISHIONERS
1919.

The Noak Hill War Memorial commemorates the men from the parish who perished during the First World War. It can be located inside St Thomas's Church in the town's aptly named Church Road. There are only nine names on the memorial, which is a godsend to know that so few from the village fell victim in the war to end all wars.

Before it started, William **Cowland** was a gardener living with his mother Elizabeth and his two elder brothers, Arthur and Charles, at Paternoster Row, Noak Hill. William enlisted in his home town of Romford and became a gunner (622304) in 'B' Battery, of the 298th (Essex) Brigade, Royal Horse Artillery and Royal Field Artillery, which was a Territorial unit.

(Photograph by Sean Connolly)

He died of his wounds on 18 September 1917 and was buried at the Divisional Collecting Post Cemetery and Extension, West-Vlaanderen, Belgium. When William was killed, the cemetery had only been open for a month, having been started by the Field Ambulance units of the 48th and 58th divisions of the British and Commonwealth Army in August 1917. We could find no record of either Arthur or Charles having served in the military during the First World War.

Arthur William **Ellingworth** and Minnie Mathews were married at Romford Parish Church on 26 October 1908. Arthur was 33 years of age at the time. Their son and only child, Eric, was born on 19 October 1910. When war broke out, Arthur knew there was every chance that he might be one of the initial tranche of men to be called up for military service, as he was an army reservist with previous military experience with the Royal Garrison Artillery. But it would be another sixteen months before he received his letter informing him that his king and country needed his service once again. He was attested on 10 December 1915 at Romford, two months past his fortieth birthday, but he wasn't mobilized until 7 March the following year and once again he found himself serving with his old regiment, the Royal Garrison Artillery, as a gunner. He was initially posted to the 22nd Battery, but on 7 September 1916 he was posted to the 20th Battery, and only four days later he was discharged from the army for 'Having been found no longer physically fit for war service' (Kings Regulation 392 (xv1). There is a note on his service record stating that he was suffering from phthisis which was 'not aggravated by service'. It is a disease that is characterized by the wasting away of the body or part of it; it is also known as pulmonary tuberculosis. He died on 5 May 1918 at the age of 43, having never recovered from his condition. He is buried in his local parish church of St Thomas, at Noak Hill.

His parents, Charles and Elizabeth Ellingworth, lived in the High Street, Romford, and his wife Minnie lived at Dagnam Park Lodge in the town.

David John **Laundy** was a lance corporal (R13418) in the 8th Battalion, Kings Royal Rifles. He enlisted on 27 June 1915 and began his training at Winchester on 1 June 1915. Once he had completed his initial training he left for Europe with his battalion, arriving in France on 17 September 1915 as part of the British Expeditionary Force. According to the 1911 census, David, along with his parents, David and Ellen, were living at Bakers Cottage, Noak Hill. They later moved on to Dace Cottage, Smiths Lane, Noak Hill, and then by 1925 his parents had moved again to 6 Church Lane, Mountnessing, Brentwood. He died on 24 August 1917. David was awarded the 1915 Star, the British War Medal and the Victory Medal for his wartime military service.

Ernest William **Laundy** enlisted at Brentwood and became a private (2476) in the 4th Battalion, Essex Regiment. The regiment sailed from Devonport on 21 July 1915 on route to Gallipoli, arriving on the peninsular at Suvla Bay on 12 August. Almost immediately the 4th Battalion were in the thick of the battle and became embroiled in some of the fiercest fighting, during which Ernest was wounded. A decision was made that his wounds were so severe that it warranted returning him to England to have them dealt with. This proved to be a journey too far for Ernest and he died of his wounds while at sea on 23 August 1915. He is buried at the East Mudros Military Cemetery in Lemnos, Greece. He was awarded the 1915 Star, as well as both the British War and Victory Medals.

Work on the East Mudros Military Cemetery began in April 1915. It contains the graves of 885 Commonwealth servicemen from the First World War, 86 of who remain unidentified. It was still being used up until September 1919. The island of Lemnos played an important role in the Gallipoli campaign against the Turkish Empire during the First World War because of its location. In preparation for the military attack on Gallipoli by Commonwealth forces, Mudros was occupied by a force of Royal Marines on 23 February 1915 and eventually became a large Allied camp. It also became a major medical facility for the treatment of Commonwealth servicemen who were wounded during the often fierce fighting on Gallipoli. It became home to the 1st and the 3rd Canadian Stationary Hospitals and the 3rd Australian General Hospital, as well as other

East Mudros Military Cemetery.
(Commonwealth War Graves Commission)

medical units, which were stationed on both sides of Mudros bay. The island would also be remembered historically as the location where the armistice between the Allies and the Turkey Empire was signed on 30 October 1918. A search for Ernest on the Commonwealth War Graves Commission website came back with a no-trace result.

Joseph and Mary Ann Ovall lived at 'Wright Bridge', Noak Hill, with their four children, William, Winnie, Jessie and Thomas, who was a 15-year-old schoolboy at the time. Soon after the war had started, Thomas **Ovall** enlisted at Warley Barracks and became a private (48324) in the 12th Battalion, East Surrey Regiment. He was killed in action on 1 October 1918. He had been born in South Weald on the outskirts of Brentwood in 1896 at the family's home. The following is the entry from the 12th Battalion's war diaries for 1 October 1918:

> *The Battalion moved at 5 am as Advance Guard for the Division in the direct of MENIN via CHELUWE. 1000 yds S.W. of CHELUWE the Battalion was held up by a strong line of M.G. Posts. Attempts to advance only partially succeeded and the Battalion suffered casualties. Lt. Edgar and 2/Lts. Targett, 2nd Lt James, Lt Bell, 2 Lt. Topham, 2/Lt. Paviour were wounded.*

It would have been during this action that Thomas was killed. Notice the naming of the six officers who were wounded but the absolute lack of any mention of men from 'the other ranks' who were also wounded. The relevance of war diaries has to be questioned when faced with such entries. When a soldier dies and is not named in person but is simply referred to as a 'casualty', it begs the question, 'why not?' Thomas was buried at the Hooge Crater Cemetery in Leper, West Vlaanderen. The crater which the cemetery is named after came about as a result of a mine detonated by the allied 3rd Division in July 1915. Hooge had been fought over many times during the course of the war and had changed hands just as often. It was regained for the final time on 28 September 1918 by the 9th (Scottish) and the 29th Divisions and held on to by the allies for the remainder of the war. There are 5,923 Commonwealth service men who were killed during the First World War buried in the cemetery, 3,579 of whom are still unidentified. Thomas was awarded the British War Medal along with the Victory Medal for his wartime service, or rather his next of kin was.

Frederick James **Stokes** was a private (14663) in the 10th Battalion,

Essex, enlisting at Warley Barracks just outside Brentwood. He died of his wounds 19 June 1918 and is buried at the Contay British Cemetery in the Somme region of France.

The Church's Roll of Honour included the following entry: **Wright**, C.G. Private 28th Ox. Bucks 22 Aug 17. A search of the Commonwealth War Graves Commission website for the surname Wright comes up with 890 possible results. If you add the initial C into the search, it comes back with only two possible results, but neither man served with the Oxford & Bucks Light Infantry. We then added the name of the regiment into the search and this came back with four possible results, but none of them had christian names beginning with the letter C, or died on 22 August 1917. We could find no trace of his Army Service record, which is not so unusual as only a small number of them survived, or any further information about him.

According to the 1911 census, Cyril Valentine **Yetton** lived at number 83, Long Lane, West Smithfield, City of London, with his parents, Thomas and Alice, and his elder brother, Thomas. He also had a sister, Hilda, who was married and was now Mrs Alcock living in East Ham. He joined the army and was a private (513031) (7013) in the 2nd/14th Battalion, London Regiment (London Scottish) as part of the Egyptian Expeditionary Force. He arrived in Salonica on 23 November 1916, was wounded in action on 8 December 1917 with a gunshot wound to the forearm, and four months later, on 30 April 1918, he was killed in action. His name is commemorated on the Jerusalem Memorial, although his service record originally stated, 'Believed to be buried in Damascus District of Syria. Grave unidentified.' It would be another six months before Mr and Mrs Yetton would receive Cyril's personal effects, which included photos, books, a cap badge, rosary beads, a crucifix and a diary, the latter being of particular interest as men from the other ranks were not allowed to keep diaries of their wartime service at the front, although a lot did. It was deemed to be such a serious offence that it was punishable by a court martial. There was not much the military authorities could do in Cyril's case though.

Arundell **Neave** was a major in the 16th (The Queens) Lancers when he was killed in action on 21 February 1915. See the plaque below about him, which can also be found inside St Thomas Church, adorning one of the walls. He is buried in the Ypres Town Cemetery along with

(Photograph by Sean Connolly)

144 other Commonwealth servicemen who fell during the bloody fighting of the First World War. From April 1915 the town was bombarded more often than any other similar sized town on the Western Front. Not surprisingly the town of Ypres was absolutely obliterated by all of the shelling, with hardly a single building being left standing. It is hard to look at the town as it is today and consider that like a phoenix, it has managed to rise from the ashes of a past life.

There is also an individual memorial to Major Arundell Neave in the Church. The inscription on it reads as follows:

Sacred to the memory of Major Arundell Neave 16th Queens Lancers, Chevalier Legion d'Honneur. 2nd son of the late Sir Arundell Neave Bart of Dagnam Park, Essex and of the Hon G G Lady Neave of Llysdulas, Anglesey. Born July 2nd 1875. Died of wounds received in action at Ypres February 21st 1915.

Fought in the Boer War 1900 to 1902. Received two medals and five clasps, mentioned in Sir John French's dispatches of October 8th 1914.

Laid to rest in the cemetery at Ypres. RIP.

CHAPTER 12

Upminster War Memorial

There are the names of sixty-six brave young men who lost their lives during the First World War on the Upminster War Memorial. The memorial was unveiled by Brigadier General C.H. de Rougemont DSO MVO on Sunday, 8 May 1921. One of his many wartime achievements saw him as the commanding officer of the Royal Heavy Artillery, 63rd Royal Naval Divisional Artillery, who were attached to the 3rd Canadian Division at the Battle of Vimy Ridge which took place on 9-12 April 1917. His wife, Muriel Evelyn de Rougemont OBE, had been the commandant of the Volunteer Aid Detachments (VADs) during the war. Their home was Coombe Lodge at Great Warley near Brentwood, which had also been a VAD hospital during the war.

Upminster had set up a war memorial committee to discuss and decide how best to remember and commemorate those men from the

(Photograph by Sean Connolly)

town who had rallied to the call to protect king and country and ended up paying the ultimate price by doing so. After much debate the decision was taken to have a war memorial designed and erected with the names on it of all of those who had fallen.

Abraham S E	**Alliston** A W	**Archer** G T
Avery C H	**Bacon** A S	**Baker** T A
Beard J C S	**Bone** E W	**Burgess** B
Burgess C H	**Butler** E W	**Caldecourt** A J
Caldecourt F R	**Cooper** L	**Coppen** H H
Coppen W J	**Cudby** F	**Curtis** R L
Dale E	**Erneston** W E	**Emerton** W T
Flack J	**Gooden** A	**Gooderham** J W
Goodwin M	**Gott** A B	**Gould** A R
Gray A B J	**Gray** G	**Hall** A R
Haynard P	**Hills** H A	**Hills** T W (MM)
Hollick J	**Hollingsworth** E H	**Horncastle** C C S
Horncastle C N	**Howard** L R	**Jupp** J W
Lavender C W	**Lee** A E	**Little** C W
Marrable W	**Marshall** E V	**Matthews** H J J

Mayes F W	**Miles** E A	**Miller** A
Moore E E	**Morrant** A	**Morrant** C
Morton W	**Nightingale** J W	**Petty** N H
Riggal C A E	**Robertson** F A	**Skilton** L W
Slocombe C J	**Smith** A H	**Sorrell** C E
Stewart S A	**Strange** J S	**Tonbridge** E
Way G C	**Webber** W T	**Wenden** W

When compared to the neighbouring Hornchurch War Memorial, there are thirteen surnames which appear on both memorials. Although not the same individuals, some of them are more than likely connected or related in some way.

A good example of this is the surname of **Marrable**, which is not a common name. If you search it on the 1911 census for the whole of England, it only comes up 321 times. Compare this against the entire population of England at the time, which was 33,847,692, it is not even one in 100,000 of the population. The name appears on the Upminster War Memorial, once with the initial W, and on the Hornchurch War Memorial it is recorded twice, with the initials J and T. From searching through the 1881, 1891, 1901 and 1911 censuses, it would appear that W stands for William and T and J stand for Thomas and James. If our research of the previous year's census is correct then it would appear that William and Thomas were brothers and Joseph was their cousin. The men's fathers, Thomas, born in 1866, and James, born in 1868, were brothers. This highlights the issue around how it was decided who was included on a particular War Memorial.

The **Hills** family had an interesting story, not just because of the Military Medal that had been awarded to their son Thomas, but also because of their collective family war effort. See what you think. Thomas William **Hills** (MM) was born in Upminster and enlisted at Basingstoke to become a private (74197) in the 113th Field Ambulance, Royal Army Medical Corps, when he died of his wounds on 16 September 1916 aged 22. Although born in Upminster he enlisted at Basingstoke. He is buried at Upminster Cemetery. The 1911 census shows the Hills family living at 'Tadlows' in Upminster. Thomas's parents, Jonathon and Eliza, had three other sons besides Thomas. Ernest was the oldest at 21. Next came Robert Charles who was 19, and their youngest son Harry William was 15. They also had a daughter who was 9.

Robert Charles **Hills** who was born on 2 April 1891 ended up enlisting in the American army in June 1917, in Harrisburg, Pennsylvania, although he had originally left England for Canada in November 1912. What is remarkable about Robert's story is that not only did he survive the First World War but he again enlisted in the American Army in the Second World War in 1943 when he was 52 years of age. At the time he was living at the Continental Hotel in Atlantic City.

Harry William **Hills** enlisted on 3 September 1914 at Stratford just after his nineteenth birthday and became a private (8086) in the 6th Battalion, Dragoon Guards, landing in France on 18 May 1915. He was awarded the 1914-1915 Star, the British War Medal and the Victory Medal. He survived the war and was finally demobilized on 30 April 1919.

We couldn't find any military records for Ernest Jonathon Hills but it is unthinkable that he wouldn't have seen military service during the war, especially as his three brothers all served and he would have only been 24 years of age at the beginning of the war.

CHAPTER 13

Trinity United Reform Church Upminster – Roll of Honour.

(Photograph by Sean Connolly)

The Trinity United Reform Church is situated on the Station Road junction with Gaynes Road in Upminster. Its architecture has a resplendent appearance as it sits peacefully inbetween a suburban residential area and the everyday hustle and bustle of a busy high street. Inside the church is a roll of honour in the form of a brass plaque on a wooden background, which commemorates those from the parish who lost their lives during the bloody battles of the First World War. There are thirteen names on the plaque, twelve of whom also appear on Upminster's main War Memorial outside St Laurence Church in Corbets Tey Road.

The only name on the above plaque which isn't also commemorated on the main Upminster War Memorial is that of A.G. **Culyer**, and his is a remarkable story. The Commonwealth War Graves Commission website shows an Alfred George **Culyer**, who originally enlisted as a private (3788) in the 1st/7th Battalion, Essex Regiment, before transferring to the 813th Area Employment Labour Company (360529) where he worked in the company quartermaster's store. He was murdered on 18 March 1919. Here is his story as well as a little of the background as to why the incident took place.

Trinity United Church Upminster and Roll of Honour.
(Sean Connolly)

Throughout the First World War, Egypt had, as a protectorate of the king, been both loyal and supportive in the war, particularly against the Ottoman Empire, but after hostilities had come to an end, she was left feeling somewhat betrayed. Whereas other peoples in the area, such as the Arabs, Palestinians and the Jews, were given some political voice, the Egyptians were not. They felt that their complaints weren't being taken seriously, if listened to at all. There was also a sense of unfairness about how they were being treated by the British in their own country. The British would requisition animals and supplies for their own military needs as and when they saw fit to do so. The local economy had not properly recovered from the war, with food prices in particular remaining at a high level. A section of Egyptian society saw one of the main reasons for this being the continued presence of the British army. Whether this was actually the case or whether it simply suited certain elements to proffer such rhetoric is a matter for debate. There was certainly a growing disaffection towards the British, almost to the point of loathing by some of the local population. On 4 April 1919 General Sir Edmund Allenby sent a telegram to Lord Curzon in London explaining the escalating and volatile nature of the situation in Egypt.

The following was taken from *Allenby in Palestine – The Middle Eastern Correspondence of Field Marshal Viscount Allenby,* edited by Matthew Hughes in 2004: On 17 March 1919, Private Alfred George Culyer, seven of his colleagues, and two British Army officers left on a train from Luxor on route to Minia. Neither the officers nor the soldiers were armed. The officers travelled in the first class carriage while Alfred and his colleagues travelled in the adjoining car. The first sign of trouble was after the train had stopped at Al Nag Hamadi when some locals boarded and proceeded to verbally abuse and insult the eight soldiers. The incident was heard by the two officers who allowed their colleagues into their first class compartment. At the next station, Assiut, three of Alfred's colleagues disembarked from the train and the Inspector of the Egyptian Prisons Department, Kaimakam Pope Bey, joined it. The train continued its journey, leaving Assiut at 4 am on 18 March 1919. The journey went from bad to worse as each stop went by. The crowds got bigger and bigger, louder and louder, and a lot more threatening in their behaviour. When the train arrived at Dairut, a large crowd attacked the train, causing the driver to flee. Sections of the crowd took over the train and started killing Alfred and his defenceless colleagues. The train stopped at Der Moes where even more crowds climbed on board the train carrying knives, sticks and stones. By the time the train arrived at Minia all of the British servicemen were dead, having been stabbed, beaten and bludgeoned to death.

Alfred is buried in the Cairo War Memorial Cemetery. He was 22 at the time of his death. He was awarded the 1915 Star, the British War Medal and the Victory Medal.

The 1911 census shows the Culyer family living at number 11 Chapel Hill, Halstead. Alfred, who was born in the town, was then a 14-year-old boy; he had left school and was an assistant draper. His only sibling was his sister Lily, aged 30. His parents, Alfred senior and Jane, were still living in Halstead at the time of Alfred's murder, which makes it somewhat unclear as to what his connection was to the Upminster area.

CHAPTER 14

All Saints Church Cranham – Roll of Honour

(Photograph Sean Connolly)

Cranham was no different to most other village communities back in the days of the First World War. When the call to arms came for young men to go off and fight for their country, seventy-nine Cranham men enlisted and took the King's shilling in payment. Nine of these brave souls did not return. To commemorate all of the village's sons, All Saints Church in Cranham not only has a roll of honour, but also has a list of the parishioners who went off to fight in the war and who were fortunate enough to return safely to their families and communities. Both lists are engraved on large brass plaques that proudly stand on the internal walls of the church. The one that has the names of those who fell during the war has the following inscription included on it:

The window close by was placed in this church by public subscription to the glory of god and in grateful remembrance of those who going forth from this parish laid down their lives in the Great War 1914 – 1919

FOR JUSTICE TRUTH AND FREEDOM. THEIR NAMES ARE UNDERWRITTEN.

William Charles **Claydon**	John **Drake**
Henry Arthur **Fishenden**	Albert Ernest **Ockendon**
Herbert Henry **Marrable**	Henry David **Kemp**
Robert Bowness **Gibson**	William Brooke **Parlby**
Thomas James **Woollard**	

Went the day well we died and never knew but well or ill, England we died for you.

Thomas James **Woollard** was a 40-year-old sergeant (17010) in the 10th Battalion, Essex Regiment when he was killed in action on 10 July 1916. He was a veteran of the Second Boer War in South Africa (1899-1902). The 10th Battalion were raised at Warley, near Brentwood, in September 1914; they then spent the next eleven months training at different locations around the country before leaving for France on 26 July 1915. A year later, on 1 July 1916, the relatively inexperienced men of the 10th Battalion would find themselves embroiled in the infamous Battle of the Somme, where the British Fourth Army incurred 50,000 casualties on the first day, 20,000 of whom were killed. The Essex Regiment had 221 men killed on the first day of the Battle of the Somme. Within two weeks that number had risen to 432. Thomas is buried at St Sever Cemetery, Rouen. There were fifteen hospitals situated in and around Rouen during the First World War, as well as a convalescent home. The majority of the dead from all of these hospitals were buried at St Sever Cemetery, which now holds 3,082 Commonwealth graves of servicemen who fell during the First World War. An interesting story about Thomas is that when his 1915 Star was issued and sent to his wife in July 1920, she had to send it back to have it amended as it showed his rank incorrectly as being that of private instead of sergeant. Thomas's widow Elizabeth lived at 'Front Lane' in Cranham along with their three sons, Albert Arthur Thomas, who was the eldest, then Robert Ernest George, and the youngest, Sidney James, who would become one of the casualties of the Second World War.

Sidney was a private (6213559) in the Middlesex Regiment. He was 25 years of age when he died on 20 October 1940, which would have made him less than a year old when his father was killed on the Western Front. The fact that Sidney is buried in All Saints Churchyard in Cranham suggests that he was wounded while serving abroad and returned to England to have his wounds treated but subsequently died.

Although he didn't serve in the Second World War, Albert would die before it had ended, passing away in May 1945 at Old Church Hospital in Romford. He left the sum of £685 in his will to his widow, Louisa.

William Charles **Claydon** was a private (G/27578) in the 13th Battalion, Duke of Cambridge's Own (Middlesex) Regiment, when he was killed in action on 31 August 1916 while serving on the Western Front. The war diaries of the 13th Battalion for the 31 August reads as follows; they were in the French town of Memetz, having arrived there late the previous day:

31 Aug 1916

Trenches knee deep in mud & blocked by troops. At 8.30am enemy bombardment commenced on all trenches – increasing up to 2pm when attack was launched – driving 'B' Coy [Company] out of TEA TRENCH and 'A' Coy back up WORCESTER TRENCH to MACDOUGAL C.T and PONT ST.

Enemy advanced to ORCHARD TRENCH where they were stopped by 2/LT GREEN with 12 men of 'D' Coy and a L.G. This party forced to retire did so in good order, holding up enemy until support could be brought up.

A Coy withdrawn from PONT ST. to CARLTON TRENCH also remnants of B & 1 platoon 'D' & 'C' Coy. Gas shells at night.

It was during this action that William was killed. In the same war diary entry was a summary of that month's casualties for the 13th Battalion. The entry showed that 9 officers and 88 men from the 'other ranks' had been killed, at an average of more than 3 per day. It also showed 17 officers and 321 other ranks had been wounded, which was nearly 11 men each day. The same timeframe also saw 146 other ranks as missing, which was more than 4 each day. All in all, this meant that the battalion was losing men at a rate of 18 each day. Replacements for the month were 11 officers and 339 other ranks, which was much less than they were losing. William is buried at the Caterpillar Valley Cemetery Longueval, in the Picardie region of France. He was awarded the British War Medal and the Victory Medal for his wartime service. The 1911 census shows him living at the Thatched House, Cranham, with his father George and his brother Frederick who was three years younger than he was. He also had two other brothers, Harry Arthur, who died in 1932 at the age of 49, and Arthur, who was born in 1893. We could find no record of either of them having served in the war. Frederick died on 27 April 1915 aged 27, but it would appear that his death was not connected to the war. He left £98 in his will to William.

Henry Arthur **Fishenden** was a signalman (London/Z/2182) in the Royal Naval Volunteer Reserve and was serving on board HMS *Racoon* when he died on 9 January 1918. HMS *Racoon* was a Beagle class destroyer that had first been launched in 1910. She was a three-funnelled coal-burning ship that had both torpedoes and medium-sized guns as part of her offensive armoury. In the early hours of 9 January 1918 she was on route from Liverpool to Lough Swilly in the Northern Approaches under the command of Lieutenant George Napier to begin convoy and anti-submarine duties. The weather at the time was appalling, with heavy seas and blizzards hampering both manoeuvrability and sight. As the ship was passing the Garvan Isles she struck rocks and sank. All ninety-one men on board, including Henry Arthur Fishenden, were lost. It is believed that he drowned in the incident. His body was never recovered and his name is commemorated on the Naval War Memorial at Chatham. It would appear that Henry's only connection to Cranham is that he worked there for a couple of years before he enlisted in the navy.

Robert Bowness **Gibson** was a 21-year-old lieutenant in the 3rd Battalion, Bedfordshire Regiment, when he was killed in action on 11 July 1916, less than two weeks into the Battle of the Somme. He is buried at the Peronne Road Cemetery, Maricourt, in the Somme. There are 1,348 Commonwealth graves in the cemetery, of soldiers who fell during the fighting on the Somme. Of these, there are 366 who are unidentified. By the end of the war Robert's parents, Thomas and Frances, were living at number 29 Linden Gardens, Bayswater, London, although the 1911 census shows them living at Cranham Rectory, Upminster, Romford, where Thomas was the parish priest. His sister Annie also lived with them, along with four servants, their daughter Barbara, and their three sons, Arthur, Paul and Geoffrey. The latter two both served in the war and survived.

John Thomas **Drake** was a corporal (3/2329) in the 10th Battalion, Essex Regiment, when he arrived in France. When he was killed in action on 21 September 1916, midway through the Battle of the Somme, he was 21 years of age. Before the war John had lived at home with his parents, George and Emily, at Ivy Cottage, North Ockendon, Essex. He had a brother, George William, who was 13, and a sister, Maud, who was 10. There was a fourth child, Lily, who was a year older than John and by 1911 was a servant for the Mallinson family who lived nearby.

John's brother George was also killed during the war. He had enlisted at Romford, where he had originally joined the Durham Light Infantry as Private 6695 before transferring to the 144th Prisoner of War Company, Labour Corps, also as a Private (374060). He died on 23 October 1918, less than three weeks before the end of the war, of broncho-pneumonia. Like his brother John, who had died two years earlier, George was 21 years of age at the time of his death. He had also previously served with the 8th Battalion, Yorkshire Regiment (41227). He is buried at the Étaples Military Cemetery in the Pas-de-Calais. It is not known why George's name is not commemorated on the same roll of honour.

Albert Ernest **Ockendon** was a private (9255) in the 1st Battalion, Essex Regiment, when he was killed in action on 4 June 1915 while fighting against the Turkish defenders at Gallipoli. Sailing from Avonmouth on 21 March 1915, he had arrived on the peninsular at Cape Helles on 25 April 1915 and almost straightaway was involved in some heavy fighting. His body was never recovered and his name is commemorated on the Helles War Memorial.

Henry David **Kemp** was born in 1892 at Woodham Walter, near Chelmsford. He was the only son of Joseph and Ellen Kemp. On enlisting in the army at Romford on 23 September 1915 he became a driver (724) in the 1st Essex Battery, Royal Horse and Field Artillery. While still in the UK he was admitted to the General Hospital in Cambridge in December 1915 due to ill health. Soon afterwards he was diagnosed with meningitis and he sadly passed away on 19 January 1915; he was 22 years of age. The 1911 census shows the Kemp family living at Tillingham Hall Cottages in nearby Chiddleditch, with Henry as an 18-year-old who worked as a cowman on one of the many local farms. Henry's sister, Ellen, who was a year older than him, had by now left home and was working as a servant for the Hansford family who lived at Westcliff-on-Sea. By the time Henry had enlisted in the army, the family had moved to Lower Cranham Road in Upminster. Henry is buried in the graveyard of his local All Saints Churchyard at Cranham. The Graves Registration Report Form of the Eastern Command (Army Division) clearly shows in red ink '(Burial fee only, paid)'. The first thought that comes to mind is that families must have been charged a fee by the army to have the body of their loved one returned to them in Cranham. It is known that the bodies of soldiers who were killed in France, regardless of their rank or family's financial status, were not allowed to be repatriated back home to them once the British Army had purchased land from the French Government to provide official cemeteries for their fallen soldiers. Orders were issued refusing all requests to have bodies exhumed and returned home to their families, regardless of the soldier's rank.

Herbert Henry **Marrable** was the oldest of five sons of Herbert and Alice Marrable who, in the 1911 census, are shown as living at number 1, Ingrebourne Cottages, Upminster. Herbert was a private (GS/51128) in the 24th Battalion, Royal Fusiliers (City of London Regiment), better known as the 2nd Sportsman's Battalion, who were stationed at the Grey Towers camp in Hornchurch from March 1915. He was killed in

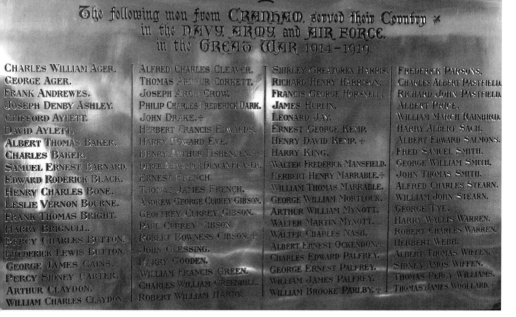

The following men from CRANHAM, served their Country in the NAVY, ARMY and AIR FORCE, in the GREAT WAR 1914-1919

CHARLES WILLIAM AGER.
GEORGE AGER.
FRANK ANDREWES.
JOSEPH DENBY ASHLEY.
CLIFFORD AYLETT.
DAVID AYLETT.
ALBERT THOMAS BAKER.
CHARLES BAKER.
SAMUEL ERNEST BARNARD.
EDWARD RODERICK BLACK.
HENRY CHARLES BONE.
LESLIE VERNON BOURNE.
FRANK THOMAS BRIGHT.
HARRY BRIGNULL.
PERCY CHARLES BUTTON.
FREDERICK LEWIS BUTTON.
GEORGE JAMES CAINS.
PERCY SIDNEY CARTER.
ARTHUR CLAYDON.
WILLIAM CHARLES CLAYDON.

ALFRED CHARLES CLEAVER.
THOMAS ARTHUR CORKETT.
JOSEPH ARCH CROW.
PHILIP CHARLES FREDERICK DARK.
JOHN DRAKE. +
HERBERT FRANCIS EDWARDS.
HARRY EDWARD EVE.
HENRY ARTHUR FISHENDEN.
DEREK ALEXANDER DUNCAN FRASER.
ERNEST FRENCH.
THOMAS JAMES FRENCH.
ANDREW GEORGE CURREY GIBSON.
GEOFFREY CURREY GIBSON.
PAUL CURREY GIBSON.
ROBERT BOWNESS GIBSON. +
JOHN GLESSING.
HARRY GOODEN.
WILLIAM FRANCIS GREEN.
CHARLES WILLIAM GREENHILL.
ROBERT WILLIAM HARDY.

SHIRLEY GREATOREX HARRIS.
RICHARD HENRY HARRISON.
FRANCIS GEORGE HORSNELL.
JAMES HURLIN.
LEONARD JAY.
ERNEST GEORGE KEMP.
HENRY DAVID KEMP. +
HARRY KING.
WALTER FREDERICK MANSFIELD.
HERBERT HENRY MARRABLE. +
WILLIAM THOMAS MARRABLE.
GEORGE WILLIAM MORTLOCK.
ARTHUR WILLIAM MYNOTT.
WALTER MARTIN MYNOTT.
WALTER CHARLES NASH.
ALBERT ERNEST OCKENDON. +
CHARLES EDWARD PALFREY.
GEORGE ERNEST PALFREY.
WILLIAM JAMES PALFREY.
WILLIAM BROOKE PARLBY. +

FREDERICK PARSONS.
CHARLES ALBERT PASTFIELD.
RICHARD JOHN PASTFIELD.
ALBERT PRICE.
WILLIAM MARCH RAINBIRD.
HARRY ALBERT SACH.
ALBERT EDWARD SALMONS.
FRED SAMUEL SMITH.
GEORGE WILLIAM SMITH.
JOHN THOMAS SMITH.
ALFRED CHARLES STEARN.
WILLIAM JOHN STEARN.
GEORGE TYE.
HARRY WALLIS WARREN.
ROBERT CHARLES WARREN.
HERBERT WEBB.
ALBERT THOMAS WIFFEN.
SIDNEY AMOS WIFFEN.
THOMAS PERCY WILLIAMS.
THOMAS JAMES WOOLLARD.

The names of those who fell are marked with a cross. (Sean Connolly)

action on 29 April 1917 during fighting in and around the French village of Gavrelle, aged 23. He has no known grave and his name is commemorated on the Arras War Memorial.

Although not mentioned on the Roll of Honour, there is a William **Marrable**, a private (51886) in the 8th Battalion, Prince of Wales's Own (West Yorkshire) Regiment, who had previously been a private (G/32458) in the Middlesex Regiment. He was killed in action on 1 September 1918 while serving on the Western Front in France. He is buried in the Vaulx Hill Cemetery in the Pas-de-Calais. We mention William as the 1901 census shows him living with his mother Susanna and her elderly parents in the All Saints Parish area, but it does give an address. The 1911 census shows the same family group living at number 1, Victoria Row, Cranham. The name W Marrable is commemorated on the Upminster War Memorial.

William Brooke **Parlby** is recorded on the Commonwealth War Graves Commission website simply as William Parlby. He was a private (9852) in the 3rd Battalion, Royal Fusiliers, when he was killed on 24 May 1915 aged 29. The 1911 census shows William Brooke Parlby and his wife Elsie May living at 115 George Street, Romford, with their 1-year-old daughter, also named Elsie. Louisa Cross, who was his sister-in-law, also lived with them. William had four sisters, Sarah, Martha, Caroline and Jessie, and an elder brother, John Chapman who, it appears, didn't serve in the war. Their father, John Potterton, died on 25 November 1905 aged 78. After the war William's mother was shown as living at 'Alysham', Harold Wood, and his widow, Elsie Mary, had moved on to Brook Cottages, High Road, in Shenfield.

CHAPTER 15

4th Battalion, Essex Regiment – Hornchurch Company

The 4th Battalion was a territorial unit of the Essex Regiment which at the start of the war in August 1914 was located in Brentwood, billeted at the Brentwood School in Middleton Hall Lane. When they were mobilized for war, the intention was for them to be used for home service, but many of the Hornchurch men volunteered for overseas service, seeing action in Gallipoli, Egypt and Palestine. The Battalion left English shores and set sail for Gallipoli on 22 July 1915. They took part in the landings at Suvla Bay on Gallipoli in August 1915 and remained on the peninsular throughout the campaign. They went on to serve in many other actions throughout the war, including the three battles of Gaza and the allied advance on Beirut.

Below is a list, taken from the 1920 publication *Hornchurch during the Great War* by Charles Thomas Perfect, of those men from the Hornchurch Company who were called up for service in early August 1914.

Major H H Slade (Promoted to lieutenant colonel in June 1916).
Lieutenant S W Williams (Transferred to RAF as a captain).
Colour Sergeant **C J Howard.**
Sergeant Instructor **H J Land.**
Sergeants **H J Bright, W Earle, G W Franklyn, H A Hunwicks and H Paul.**
Lance Sergeant **C H Baker.**

Corporals **A G Collin, L W Earl, B F Ward, C Newman, and R S Wicks.**

Lance Corporals **H B Bush, E G Everson, W C Gower, A E Monk, and W R Stamp.**

Bandsman **C H Barlow.**

Drummer **C E Bond.**

Privates W Abrams, W Barlow, J Brockhurst, A T Burrell, W C Blows, C Banks, F T Bright, C Coulson, P E Coulson, E Clarke, H Clark, C Cook, E Cook, A B Claxton, S Cosby, E H Dunk, R A Dunk, R Dare, A Dawson, A Ellis, H A Franklyn, J G Franklyn, F M Francis, T G Frost, W Guy, A W Gentry, W H Grey, E Garrett, E E Hill, G Hurrell, A R Hutson, D J Hutson, S E Hardy, C F Hardy, H Hills, J Harris, B Knight, F J Kemp, P Livermore, B Lake, J London, W H London, W Lovell, L Lowe, F Martin, W Minns, T H Mills, C Newman, G G Newman, G North, H H Ollington, J W Oldham, R Pemberton, W A Parish, H Pridgeon, A T Perry, W A Promfrett, C W Purkiss, G Rogers, W Stebbing, C G Smith, L A Says, E Tucker, F Talbot, H G Tibble, R G Tyler, A J Thompson, W Ticker, A H Wall, H Wall, S Wall, J Wood, H Woods, G J Ward, D S Wellinton, J S Whatling, W A Warman, L Westgate.

Boys H Eady, C W Huxtable, F R Steadman.

The above list isn't a comprehensive list of all of those who served with Hornchurch Company of the 4th Battalion, Essex Regiment, simply a list of those men who were called up at the very start of the war.

Records show that the 4th Battalion lost a total of 347 men who were either killed in action, died of their wounds, or who fell victim to illness while serving with the battalion during the First World War. This doesn't include those men who initially joined the 4th Battalion and then transferred elsewhere within the regiment or to other fighting military units. Those men who died after having transferred from the 4th Battalion, will have been recorded separately on their subsequent battalion, regiment, corps or unit's records.

Of those who fell, thirty-five were men who were either born, enlisted or lived in the Hornchurch, Romford, or Upminster areas, twenty-one of these were killed during the fighting of the First Battle of Gaza. On 26 March 1917, British forces had to advance across open and exposed ground as they attacked Turkish positions, with only luck on their side to determine who amongst them would fall victim to artillery shells, machine gun fire or snipers' bullets. After gaining a foothold in the Turkish defences, an effort which had resulted in some 3,500 British casualties, their commander decided to call off the attack as the early evening skies began to darken.

Private 200335 William **Abrams** was killed in action in Palestine on 27 March 1917. He enlisted at Rainham.

Private 200961 Arthur John **Ashwell** was killed in action on 27 March 1917 in Palestine. Before the war he had lived at Wennington.

Company Quarter Master Sergeant Charles Henry **Baker** died of his wounds while at sea on his way back to England on 24 August 1915. He was born, enlisted and lived at Hornchurch.

Private 200637 Thomas Arthur **Baker** was killed in action on 27 March 1917 in Palestine. He was born and enlisted at Upminster.

Private 200320 Frank Henry **Bull** was killed in action on 26 March 1917 in Palestine. He was born in Hornchurch.

Private 201060 Frederick William **Collin** was killed in action on 25 March 1917 in Palestine. Before the war he had lived in Hornchurch.

Private 200676 Marshall **Cook** was killed in action on 26 March 1917 in Palestine. Before the war he had lived in Romford.

Private 33109 Charles John **Eary** died of his wounds on 11 December 1917 in Palestine. He was born and lived in Romford.

Sergeant 200118 Timothy Gibson **Frost** was killed in action on 3 November 1917 in Palestine. He was born, enlisted and lived in Hornchurch.

Private 3472 Bertie Robert **Fry** died at Aylesbury Military Hospital on 4 April 1917, suggesting that he either died as a result of his wounds he had received while fighting in Palestine, or from some kind of illness he had contracted. Prior to the war he had lived at Primrose Villa, North Street, Hornchurch.

Private 200089 William **Guy** died of his wounds on 27 March 1917 in Palestine. He was born in Hornchurch and enlisted and lived at Harold Wood.

Company Sergeant Major 200035 Harry William **Hale** was killed in action on 3 November 1917 in Palestine. He had enlisted and lived in Romford before the war.

Private 200897 Thomas George **Holmes** died of his wounds on 27 March 1917 in Palestine. He had enlisted and lived in Romford before the war.

Private 200582 John Henry **Howell** was killed in action on 26 March 1917 in Palestine. Before the war he had enlisted and lived in Hornchurch.

Private 1577 Charles William **Huxtable** was killed in action on 23 August 1915 in Gallipoli. He was born in Romford and enlisted at Hornchurch.

Corporal 200258 William Thomas **Muckleston** was killed in action on 26 March 1917 in Palestine. He was born in Hornchurch.

Private 200786 Harry **Palmer** was killed in action 26 March 1917 in Palestine. Before the war he lived in Romford.

Private 200144 Albert Thomas **Perry** was killed in action on 26 March 1917 in Palestine. Before the war he had enlisted at Hornchurch.

Private 201307 George **Phillips** was killed in action on 26 March 1917 in Palestine. Before the war he had been living in Wennington.

Private 2244 Bertie Stanley **Prior** was killed in action on 13 September 1915 at Gallipoli. Before the war he had lived at Romford.

Corporal 200579 William Ernest **Purkis** was killed in action on 1 May 1918 at Gallipoli. Before the war he had lived and enlisted at Hornchurch.

Private 2272 Jesse William **Ramsey** died on 30 September 1915 while serving in Egypt. Before the war he had lived in Romford.

Private 1993 Frederick Robert **Raymond** died on 16 October 1916 while serving in Egypt. Before the war he had lived and enlisted at Romford.

Private 200181 Sydney Edgar **Saunders** had died of his wounds at home on 5 January 1918. He was born, had enlisted and lived in Romford. There is no record of Sydney on the Commonwealth war Graves Commission website.

Private 2623 Alexander **Scott** died at sea on 12 October 1915, which could possibly indicate that he had been wounded in battle and that he died of his wounds while on his way back to England.

Private 200871 Walter **Scott** died of his wounds on 27 March 1917 while serving in Palestine. Prior to the war he had lived in Romford.

Private 201260 Stephen **Shaw** was killed in action on 26 March 1917 while serving in Palestine. Before the war he had enlisted at Romford.

Private 200636 William **Smoothy** was killed in action on 27 March 1917 while serving in Palestine. Before the war he had enlisted and lived at Upminster.

Private 201265 Harry William **Thorogood** was killed in action on 27 March 1917 while serving in Palestine. He was born and enlisted at Romford and before the war he had lived at Hornchurch.

Private 200353 Richard George **Tyler** died of his wounds on 27 March 1917 while serving in Palestine. He was born, enlisted and lived in Hornchurch.

Acting Sergeant 747 Basil Frank **Ward** was killed in action on 20 August 1915 while serving in the Gallipoli campaign. He had enlisted at Hornchurch.

Private 200254 George **Warman** was killed in action on 27 March 1917 while serving in Palestine. He was born, lived and enlisted at Romford.

Sergeant 200255 David Stephen **Wellington** was killed in action on 27 March 1917 while serving in Palestine. He had enlisted at Hornchurch.

Lance Corporal Wilfred Aubrey **Wraight** was killed in action on 25

November 1917 while serving in Palestine. Prior to the war he had lived in Romford.

Private 200180 William James **York** was killed in action on 27 March 1917 while serving in Palestine. He was born, enlisted and lived in Romford.

CHAPTER 16

Church Lads' Brigade – Hornchurch

The Church Lads' Brigade was a national organization set up in 1891 for the benefit of local youths aged between 13 and 19, to give them a purpose, discipline and an inner desire to make something of themselves in their adult lives, as well as providing them with bible classes for their religious instruction.

The Hornchurch section was set up on 30 September 1903, the year after the end of the Second Boer War in Africa, and at a time when military discipline was still very much part of everyday life, which was possibly why one of the brigade's main objectives was to train its members in the principles of military exercises.

To add to the disciplined nature of the brigade, the boys wore a military style uniform which consisted of a forage cap, a belt, what today would be called a rucksack but in pre-war Britain was referred to as a haversack, and a carbine.

A total of eighty-eight young men who had served with the Hornchurch Section of the Church Lads' Brigade would go off to fight in the war; eight of them didn't come home.

Walter **Cressey** was a private (34131) in the 9th Battalion, Essex Regiment, when he was killed on 9 April 1917. He was 23 years of age. He has no known grave and his name is commemorated on the Arras War Memorial.

Ernest Walter **Nicholls** was a stoker 1st class in the Royal Navy on board HMS *Arethusa* when he died, aged 20, on 11 February 1916.

HMS *Arethusa* was a light cruiser and was the only one of her class sunk during the First World War. She took part in the Battle of Heligoland Bight on 28 August 1914, which was the first significant naval action of the war in the North Sea. She was badly damaged during the battle and had to be towed back to Harwich having lost eleven of her crew dead and a further seventeen wounded. After repairs were carried out on her, the next significant action she saw was at Dogger Bank on 24 January 1915, when she struck the German cruiser *Blücher* with two torpedoes, returning later to pick up survivors. On 11 February 1916 *Arethusa* struck a mine in the shipping lanes just off Felixstowe, which had only been laid the previous day by the German submarine *UC7*. Six of the *Arethusa*'s crew, including Ernest Nicholls, were killed in the subsequent explosion. The ship was finished, first running aground and subsequently breaking up on the rocks. Ernest's body was never recovered. His name is commemorated on the Chatham Naval Memorial.

Percy Alexander **Dunlop** originally enlisted as a private (2939) in the 2nd Battalion, London Scottish Regiment. Despite at 39 years of age not having to enlist, he did so on 2 September 1914 at Westminster, with the war less than a month old. He would later transfer to the 14th Battalion of the same regiment, before transferring to the Labour Corps and becoming a lance corporal. During the war he had served in Dublin, dealing with the Irish Rebellion of August 1915. He also served in France, Macedonia and Salonika, where he died in the 63rd General Hospital on the 28 October 1918, not of wounds received in battle, but because he had contracted malaria and nephritis. He is buried at the Mikra British Cemetery in Salonika. He was 43 years of age at the time of his death. Prior to enlisting in the army, Percy had been a lieutenant in the Hornchurch Company of the Church Lads' Brigade, even though at the time of his death his home address was shown as being at number 13, Ramuz Drive, Westcliff-on-Sea, where he lived with his wife Bertha and their 13-year-old daughter Eileen. His job as a printer manager saw them wealthy enough to be able to afford a servant.

According to the 1911 census John Edward **Gaywood** was 14 years of age and lived in the High Street, Hornchurch, with his parents, John and Constance, and his 6-year-old sister, Louisa. By this time John had already left school and was bringing money into the home by working as a clerk at Hornchurch Railway Station. John was an acting bombardier (340651) in the Royal Garrison Artillery when he was killed in the early part of 1917 at just 21 years of age. He was awarded the British War Medal and the Victory Medal for his wartime service.

When James Rueben **Hawkins** originally enlisted in the army at Upminster on 10 August 1916 he had just turned 18. He became a private (5459) in the 6th Battalion, Durham Light Infantry, at Catterick Bridge. On 14 October 1916 he transferred to the 2nd/1st Battalion, Yorkshire Hussars, as private 3588/330880 at Bridlington, before transferring to the 3rd Battalion, Prince of Wales's Own (West Yorkshire) Regiment where he became private 77870. He was then sent to France where he arrived on 31 August 1918, joining the 10th Battalion of the same regiment. He had been in France for only three days when on the night of 3/4 September 1918 he was killed in action. His family's home at the end of the war was 'Emsworth', Parkstone Avenue, Hornchurch, but in the 1911 census they lived at 'Parkstone', Pole Road, Emerson Street, Hornchurch. His parents, James and Susannah, had three other children, Edward who was 8, Susannah 17, and the baby of the family was 6-year-old Dorothy.

John Dane **Hammond** was a lance corporal (17887) in the 2nd Battalion, Norfolk Regiment when he died of his wounds on 23 April 1916. His name is commemorated on the Basra War Memorial in Iraq, which includes the names of more than 40,000 Commonwealth soldiers who died while serving in Mesopotamia from the latter part of 1914 through till the end of August 1921. The memorial was unveiled on 27 March 1929 by Sir Gilbert Clayton.

William George **Hammond** enlisted on 18 June 1915 at Romford as a rifleman (C/6048) in the 18th (Service) Battalion (Arts & Crafts), Kings Royal Rifle Corps. The battalion had been raised at Gidea Park on 4 June 1915 by Major Sir Herbert Raphael and landed in France on 4 May 1916. Six weeks later, he was killed, on 30 June 1916. His parents, George and Alice, lived at number 6, St James Cottages, Brentwood Road, Romford.

Harold Allfrey **Taylor** was a corporal (19411) in the 26th (Bankers) Battalion, Royal Fusiliers. A native of Hornchurch, he was 25 years of age when he was killed on 7 June 1917. At the end of the war his parents, Frederick and Minnie, were living at the Old Bank House, 42

Leigh Hill, Leigh-on-Sea. He is buried at the Voormezeele Enclosure No.3, West-Vlaanderen.

Over the years many boys were part of the brigade and an estimated 250,000 of them went off to serve their king and country during the years of the First World War. Ex-Brigade boys would go on to win 13 Victoria Crosses, 72 Military Crosses and 199 Military Medals for their acts of bravery.

The brigade's patron saint is St Martin of Tours who died on 8 November 397. He was the Bishop of Tours in France and would go on to become one of the most familiar and recognizable Christian saints of all time. As legend would have it, he was conscripted into the Roman army as a young man, following in the footsteps of his father who was a tribune in the Imperial Horse Guard, a unit of the Roman army. Martin found being a soldier was incompatible with his Christian faith and became a conscientious objector. A banner which depicts St Martin hangs in Westminster Abbey. It was presented by the Brigade in 1921 to honour its members who had died during the First World War.

CHAPTER 17

Romford in the
Eyes of the Press

Even with the restrictions that were placed on the press throughout the war by legislation which was brought in by Government, mainly by the Defence of the Realm Act, some record of events did make it into both local and national newspapers and other publications.

In this chapter we look at the war and its effects both at home and abroad as seen and recorded in the pages of the beleaguered press.

Two of the better known weekly newspapers which covered the Romford and Brentwood areas were the *Chelmsford Chronicle* and the *Essex Newsman*. Below are some of the articles which they reported on during the war years:

1914

Chelmsford Chronicle Friday, 14 August 1914.

Hornchurch War Committee

A public meeting convened by the Chairman of the Hornchurch Parish Council and the Reverend Herbert Dale, vicar of Hornchurch, was held at Hornchurch. Mr W H Legg presided.

The Reverend Herbert Dale suggested that people should come forward and offer to take in and care for the wounded or sick, after convalescence.

In the same edition of the newspaper was the confirmation that Britain being at war with Germany was already having an effect on the home front.

Romford Relief Committee

Last night a public meeting, convened by Mr E Winmill, JP and Chairman of the Romford Urban Council, was held at the Drill Hall.

Mr Winmill suggested a war relief fund, collected and administrated in such a way that there was no overlapping.

Sir Montagu Turner proposed that a fund is formed. The money could be obtained locally, and, if so desired, sent to the Prince of Wales Fund, which would make grants to the district, for the local committee to administer. They should represent the Romford district, and ask any existing societies, like the Red Cross, to come in and work for them.

The meeting provoked much discussion on the topic of what the monies that were collected should be spent on. One idea was to pass it on to the Prince of Wales Fund, another to provide clothing for the local Territorial Battalion of the Essex Regiment, while another suggested it should be 'for the relief of immediate necessities'. There was also the suggestion of working in conjunction with surrounding areas such as Havering and Hornchurch and getting everybody to donate to the fund. Reading through the article it wasn't clear what the fund was actually needed for. It certainly didn't appear that there was a clear or specific need. It seemed to be more about collecting monies from an already poverty-stricken local population and then coming up with ideas on how the fund could best be spent.

The war had certainly stirred up a national fervour coupled with a desire to 'do ones bit for the war effort', usually by those who were either too old or infirm to go off and actually fight.

Reading through copies of the *Chelmsford Chronicle* and the *Essex Newsman* weekly newspapers for September 1914 brought with it a surreal feeling. There was not one single major headline about the war in a local capacity. For sure there were general snippets of information which recounted stories from across Essex, but there was little to be found in relation to Romford and its surrounding areas.

A desire to join the Sportsman's Battalion had caught the imagination of the general public:

Chelmsford Chronicle Friday, 16 October 1914

Sportsman's Battalion at Hornchurch

The newly formed 'Sportsman's Battalion' have begun their training at Grey Towers Park, Hornchurch, this week. A great deal of temporary accommodation has been erected in the park for their convenience. At the meeting of the Romford Rural District Council on Tuesday reference was made to the fact that one of the 'huts' of the battalion obstructed a public footpath. It was pointed out by Mr Blatchell that the deviation caused was about a yard, and no action was taken.

Chelmsford Chronicle Friday, 6 November 1914

Sportman's Battalion at Hornchurch

On Wednesday the Sportsman's Battalion arrived at Romford by train from London, and marched to their encampment at Grey Towers, Hornchurch. The battalion, who were under the command of Lord Maitland, were accorded a hearty welcome at Romford, being met at the station by a large crowd. The band of the Hornchurch Cottage Homes, under Bandmaster H W Alden, placed themselves at the head of the battalion, and played martial airs along the road to Hornchurch.

Extensive preparations have been made at Hornchurch for the reception of the battalion during their training, which should be shortened by the effective character of the men comprising it, to most of whom shooting is a familiar pastime.

Word of what was fast becoming one of the most prestigious regiments in the British army had already spread far and wide, as can be confirmed by the following report from the Scottish Press:

Aberdeen Journal Friday, 16 October 1914

Recruiting in Scotland for Sportsman's Battalion

Starting from Monday next, recruiting will begin throughout Scotland for the Sportsman's Battalion, Royal Fusiliers (City of

London Regiment), which has been recruiting at the hotel Cecil in London. Officers will attend at recruiting stations at Edinburgh, Aberdeen and Inverness, as there are still a few vacancies for this first rate regiment for the right kind of men, sportsmen of fine physique, thoroughly sound and fit, up to 45; height preferred 5ft 11in. and upwards. This is the only Corps for which the War Office has specially extended the age limit to 45.

The Corps is an infantry one, with the ordinary infantry training, and the medical examination. Pay at Army rates. Payment by the recruit for his equipment is optional. He need not be put to any expense if he does not wish. The officer commanding is Viscount Maitland.

The headquarters of the Corps are at the Grey Towers, Hornchurch near Romford, Essex. Further particulars will immediately be announced.

There was a certain irony in the part of the article that spoke about those wishing to join the regiment having the option to buy and pay for all of their equipment. Here were a select group of brave young men prepared to go off and fight for their king and country in a war in some far-off foreign land, and as if that wasn't going to be traumatic enough, they were also being given the option of paying for their own equipment.

The Essex County Chronicle Friday, 20 November 1914

Mr Charles Watkins, missionary and probation officer at East Ham, Romford, Saffron Walden, Stansted and Harlow Police Courts, has received an appointment as Lieutenant and adjutant on the Salisbury Army Staff. He has two sons with the Colours, Forbes in the Suffolk Yeomanry, and Charles in the Civil Service Rifles. His youngest son, Ernest, belongs to the Leytonstone National Volunteer Reserve.

There is a very sad story attached to this article which is not immediately obvious. The first point that stuck out about it was how an ordinary member of the general public had simply been drafted into the army as an officer without any military experience whatsoever. That just didn't seem right. Armed with the knowledge that Charles Watkins had three sons, the research could begin. The first place we looked was on the Commonwealth War Graves Commission website which showed that a Charles Watkins, aged 47, who was a lieutenant on the general list, had died on 30 January 1915 and that he was buried at the City of London Cemetery and Crematorium at Manor Park. The fact that he was buried in England also confirmed that is where he had died. His cause of death is not known. What the information also confirmed was that Charles had previous military experience, having served with the Gordon Highlanders in the Second Boer War in South Africa (1899-1902). He had also been awarded the King Edward Coronation Medal as well as the Long Service and Good Conduct Medal, indicating he had served in the military for over twenty years. The entry also showed that he lived at 145 Whipps Cross Road, Leytonstone, which is where his youngest son Ernest was in the National Volunteer Reserve, and that his wife was J.A. Watkins. A check on the 1911 census showed a Charles who was 43 years of age, Jane Ann who was 42, Forbes who was 17, Charles who was 16, and Ernest who was 13. Their daughter Olive was 14. It was definitely the same Charles Watkins who was mentioned in the newspaper article. The address shown on the 1911 census is 30 Bruce Grove, Tottenham, but it has to be remembered that the address shown on the Commonwealth War Graves Commission website would have been posted more than ten years after the one shown on the 1911 census. Both Forbes and Charles junior survived the war, with Forbes eventually emigrating to Canada, arriving in Sandwich, Ontario by boat on 5 October 1932. Ernest, like his father, wasn't so fortunate. He followed his brother Charles into the London Regiment (Prince of Wales's Own Civil Service Rifles) as Private 3721 in the 1st/15th Battalion. At the time of his death on Christmas Eve 1916 he was attached to the 140th Trench Mortar Battery. He is buried at Woods Cemetery which is situated in the Leper, West Vlaanderen region of Belgium.

With the fighting in the early stages of the war centring on Belgium, it wasn't going to be too long before refugees started arriving in Britain in their efforts to escape the troubles:

Essex Newsman Saturday, 24 October 1914

Belgian Refugees

A party of five Belgian refugees from Ostend, consisting of a mother and four daughters, arrived at Romford on Tuesday evening. They are accommodated in rooms above St. Edwards Girls School room. Another family, a party of four, consisting of four, consisting of father, mother and two children, are expected at Romford. They will be accommodated at the Vicarage until other arrangements are made. Sir Herbert Raphael Bart, MP, has lent Balgores House, Gidea Park, for the accommodation of refugees.

The topic of Special Constables had become somewhat of a prickly political issue. Their original purpose was to have a body of men to cover for those full-time serving police officers who had gone off to fight in the war, and to effectively supplement the numbers of those who were left. It quickly became obvious in most social circles that one way to avoid enlisting in the army and being sent off to war was to volunteer to become a Special Constable. But in the following articles, there is no hint of that:

Essex Newsman Saturday, 3 October 1914

Special Constables

Parades of Special Constables who have been sworn in for duty in Romford and the adjacent Parishes, took place on Monday evening at Romford, Hornchurch, Upminster and Gidea Park. In all there are about 300 Special Constables in the district. The parades were inspected by Mr Burnett Tabrum, JP, and the Special Constables were supplied with truncheons, armlets, whistles and warrant cards. Mr Tabrum expressed his pleasure at the ready response they had made to the appeal to those willing to serve. Supt. Mules of Romford addressed the Special Constables at each of the parades. He explained their duties and powers, expressing the pleasure he felt at having them to assist in the protection of life and property. The Police of the Romford Division felt a great indebtedness to Mr Burnett Tabrum and his son, who had devoted a tremendous amount of time and energy to the organisation of the Special Constables.

Captain Ffinch and the Romford Special Constables

At Romford on Sunday the Special Constables for the Romford

District, which includes Gidea Park, Harold Wood, Hornchurch and Upminster, paraded at the Football Ground, Romford, and were inspected by Captain Ffinch, who was accompanied by Mr Burnett Tabrum, JP, and Mr Percy Tabrum. The Special Constables, who numbered about 200, went through various drill exercises.

Addressing the parade at the conclusion of these movements, Capt. Ffinch complimented the men on the way in which they had carried out their evolutions. There were one or two faults, which a little time and practice would remedy. He knew that many people thought drills were not necessary for Special Constables, but as there is a possibility of their being called in to assist civil Police and the military, he thought drills were absolutely necessary, as otherwise they would not be of much value in co-operation. There were also people who said that Special Constables were not required, but in the view of the Government, the Chief Constable, and of many far-seeing people, they were necessary.

He congratulated the men of Romford on coming forward in such numbers, and pointed out that there was a great deal of valuable property requiring close attention, and that the people would be very grateful for the assistance they were rendering. It was not for every man to go to the front, many of them had family and business ties, but if they did their duty in this way he was sure they would earn the gratitude of the country.

He would be seeing Capt. Showers, the Chief Constable, very shortly, and would inform him of the fine body of men there was at Romford. In conclusion, he would like to express thanks to Mr Bennett Tabrum and his son for the great assistance they had rendered to the movement.

The following is an interesting article about a returning wounded Romford soldier:

Chelmsford Chronicle Friday, 6 November 1914

Essex Wounded

Pt. Alfred Saitch, of Clifton Road Romford, who was wounded in the arm at the Battle of the Aisne while serving with the 2nd

Grenadier Guards, has arrived home. The enemy were seen approaching with the white flag. The British went forward to capture them, whereupon the Germans opened fired. While extricating his bayonet from a German, Saitch was wounded in the left arm by a Maxim gun shot.

With the war now some four months old (November 1914) it is noticeable that there are longer and longer lists appearing in the local newspapers of those who have been killed at the front. The Royal Fusiliers paid a heavy price for doing their duty for king and country; by the time the war was over they had lost a staggering 17,757 men in the bloody and brutal fighting of the war.

Soldiers knew only too well the inherent dangers which went with the job they did, especially in a time of war, but most would take it as a given that while back home in the relevant safety of their barracks in England, any such risks wouldn't be so apparent. Well, you would think that would be the case, wouldn't you? Read on:

Essex Newsman Saturday, 28 November 1914

Accident

On Saturday night Pt. C Hanbury of the Sportman's Battalion, was riding a motor bicycle towards Hornchurch when he collided with a horse drawing a cab. The horse fell upon the soldier and his machine. Hanbury was extricated by some comrades and taken to the camp hospital (Grey Towers).

There was no mention in the article about what happened to the poor old horse or explanation as to how Private Hanbury managed not to see the horse merrily making its way slowly along the road while pulling a cab.

1915

The following article showed just how quickly an incident could mushroom out of control, with it not being entirely clear from where the original information had come. What it did show was that the plans the authorities had in place to deal with such emergencies, worked effectively:

The Birmingham Daily Mail Tuesday, 2 February 1915

Air Raid scares over London

Authorities Precautions

For two hours last night London was busy with rumours to the effect that a fleet of Zeppelins were on their way to the Metropolis. How the rumour originated is something of a mystery, but within a short time it was very general, and the Exchange Company received enquiries from all parts of London. One enquirer had heard that no less than five of the Kaiser's airships were on their way from Hornchurch and other enquiries gave varying numbers.

The Romford and Hornchurch Police treated the matter as a joke, and telephone calls to Harwich, Cromer, Southend, Tilbury, Ipswich, Grimsby, Sheringham, King's Lynn, Yarmouth, Hull, Colchester, and other places elicited the reply in each case that all was quiet and that no raiders had been seen.

The authorities in London, however, were evidently determined to leave nothing to chance. At certain railway stations lights were either put out altogether or considerably diminished, and trains passing over the bridges did so in darkness. The authorities at Scotland Yard were soon on the alert, and Special Constables were told to report themselves at headquarters. The telephone exchanges were kept busy for more than two hours with subscribers anxious to know the latest.

The following is a story of Romford heroism:

The Essex County Chronicle Friday, 9 April 1915

Romford Man's Brave Deed

The Territorial NCO, the story of whose gallant action in rescuing a wounded officer in the face of the enemy's fire, has been widely circulated, proves to be Sergeant Ravan of the Hertfordshire Battalion, who formerly lived in Waterloo Road, Romford.

During a spirited charge, a number of the King's Royal Rifles were caught in a concealed German trench, over which was barbed wire covered with earth. At the same time, the Germans opened a heavy fire on them from machine guns and also shelled them with petrol bombs.

> *When the Hertfordshires relieved the Rifles four days later a wounded officer was seen in an exposed position. At night Sergeant Ravan went out at great risk from flying bullets and brought in the officer.*

Essex Newsman Saturday, 21 August 1915

Took Leave

> *James Gregory, a Private of the 15th Battalion King's Royal Rifles, stationed at Belhus Park, Aveley, was charged on Wednesday with being absent without leave since August 10. PC Reynolds said he arrested the prisoner at Hornchurch. He stated that he could not get leave, so he took it. Remanded to wait an escort.*

One wonders if Private Gregory would have been so flippant or maverick in his approach and attitude if he had been serving in France at the time of his need to take leave, an act that would have no doubt seen him standing in front of a court martial facing the possibility of a firing squad for desertion. Checking the Commonwealth War Graves Commission website there are six men who were killed during the First World War with the name J Gregory who also served with the King's Royal Rifle Corps, three of whom we know had the Christian name of James. None of them served in the 15th Battalion, but a month after this matter, on September 25 1915, Rifleman 12195, James Gregory, who was 18 years of age, was killed while serving in Belgium with the 9th Battalion of the King's Royal Rifle Corps. Is this one and the same person?

Here is a strange story of human weakness that came before the district court:

Essex Newsman Saturday, 2 October 1915

Romford Sept 30

A Broken Romance

> *Pt. Barnard Towse, 30th (Reserve) Battalion, Royal Fusiliers, was charged on remand with stealing a military mackintosh, value £3, and a lady's gold watch and chain, value £5, of Florence Amy Paterson, Easton Road, Romford. Amy Paterson, a school teacher,*

daughter of the prosecutrix, said she made the acquaintance of the prisoner about 5 weeks ago, at the Hare Street Camp, he having rescued her little dog, which had been nearly run over. She had since seen him on several occasions at her mother's house.

The prisoner, who made no statement, was committed for trial at the next quarter session.

While men were abroad fighting for king and country, life was still going on back home as normally as it possibly could in the circumstances, but if one looked deep enough there was nearly always a connection to the war in any given situation. The next article highlights this point:

Chelmsford Chronicle Friday, 24 December 1915

Romford Workhouse

At Romford Workhouse the special feature of the Christmas festivities is the participation by the wounded soldiers, of whom a number are being treated in the Hospital. The soldiers who are at Marshalls Park are also being entertained, special provision having been made for bringing these men to Romford to join their comrades for Christmas. On Christmas Day there will be the usual service with carols, conducted by the Chaplain, the Rev. H R Phillpots. The inmates, who number about 450, will enjoy a special Christmas dinner of roast pork, beef and mutton, vegetables, and plum pudding, with coffee and mineral waters, but no beer. There will also be nuts, oranges, apples, and tobacco. For tea there will be extra cake. In the evening a concert and entertainment will be given, the programme being arranged by the Master, Mr A Hesford, who, with the Matron and the staff, has done all in his power to ensure a happy Christmas for his charges.

During the First World War, certainly the early stages of it, there was no such thing as a welfare state or an old age pension. When somebody was past the age of being able to work, or simply couldn't work due to poor health, and had no immediate family who were able to provide for them, it was a life in the local workhouse that beckoned.

Times have changed somewhat and the health risks connected to the pastime of smoking are more known about now than they were in 1915. When the wars in Iraq and Afghanistan were in full swing between 2001 and 2015, there was a desire, almost a need to send parcels to the troops, providing those back home with a feeling of wellbeing, whether they were a friend or relative, but there was no official or public drive to send tobacco and cigarettes:

A Duty for those at Home

All of us know what a soldier's duty is, but do we all realize what is the duty of those not in khaki? Whether we are over age, medically unfit, or members of the weaker sex, we too have a duty, and one which is just as important in its way as the duty of the soldier or sailor, who takes the King's shilling. That duty is to see that those who are fighting for us are not forgotten, and that they get whatever we can afford in the way of little luxuries. One of the few luxuries that Tommy has an opportunity of enjoying is the chance to have a good smoke. There is nothing more mistaken than the view that because a thing is serious you must be thinking about it seriously all the time. Tommy Atkins has some serious things to do and to think about, but he has some moments of semi-leisure, when anything that takes his mind off the thing he has on hand affords him the greatest enjoyment. Something to smoke fills this want admirably.

A soldier recently returned from the front was asked by a friend whether he found tobacco helped him much. His answer was that they simply could not do without it. 'When a chap is badly hit,' he said, 'we simply shove a lighted fag in his mouth, and he does not care a rap about anything. If it was not for the tobacco we would all be dead, and you may well guess a trench is not a nice sweet scented place.'

So don't forget to see first of all that your friend or relative at the front has plenty to smoke, and don't forget those also who have no friends at home sufficiently in a position to be able to afford to send them anything like a regular supply.

The following remarkable story is about an old war hero on his way to visit his nephew who was a latter day version of himself:

Chelmsford Chronicle Friday, 31 December 1915

Upminster – Sailor's Illness

On Tuesday night PC Beseley was at the railway station, when he heard cries for help coming from the subway. He found Foreman-Porter Roach with a man who was lying on the floor in a fit. Upon the advice of the Station-master, Mr Wallace, the man was removed to a room and seen by Dr Bletsoe, who said he was suffering from malaria and ague. He was conveyed to the Romford Infirmary. A seaman's discharge papers found on the man showed that he was John Iverson of Gravesend. He stated that he was on his way to the Romford Military Hospital to see a wounded nephew. He had a cork leg, having lost a limb during the relief of Ladysmith, when he was serving with HMS Powerful's *crew on land.*

The reference to the relief of Ladysmith was in connection to an event which occurred during the Second Boer War in South Africa (1899-1902) when British forces led by Lord Dundonald with a young Winston Churchill by his side entered Ladysmith on the afternoon of 1 March 1900, finally ending the Boers' siege of the town.

1916

Here is a story about the blackout:

Chelmsford Chronicle Friday, 25 February 1916

Upminster Man and 'Zepps'

Yesterday, at Romford, Douglas Brooking Sanders, gentleman, Great Tompkins, Bird Lane, Upminster, was summonsed for not reducing certain lights or screening his windows.

PS Beasley said that on February 11 he was on duty near defendant's premises when he saw bright lights shining from the windows. The lights were acetylene, and could be seen for miles away, as the house stood on a hill near the Common. There were practically no blinds and he could tell the time by his watch thirty yards off. Defendant told witness he was aware of the Lighting Order, but he thought the lighting restrictions were ridiculous, because Zeppelins would not come to a sparsely populated district like Upminster.

Defendant did not appear and Inspector Howlett said the Police regarded this as a very bad case.

The Chairman (Mr Henry Joslin) said the case had several bad features. Defendant was not present; he did not confess his fault and say he would mend his ways; and altogether he had set the law at defiance. He would be fined £2 and the penalty would be heavier if any further complaints were received.

A regular event of the war were the exemption tribunals which took place up and down the country whereby men of all ages and commitments, tried to be excused military service. The tribunals usually consisted of a local Justice of the Peace, four other pillars of the local community, a clerk, and a military representative.

Chelmsford Chronicle Friday, 10 March 1916

A Solicitor's Application

Edward H Hawkins, bricklayer, Dagenham, applied for exemption on the ground he was the sole support of his home, and his employer, Mr Earle, also applied for the exemption on the ground that the man was indispensable. Mr Earle said Hawkins was the only jobbing bricklayer in Dagenham. The application of the man was dismissed, but two months' exemption was allowed on the application of the employer.

Other applications heard at the same tribunal included that of a milkman, a stockman, a solicitor, and a conscientious objector. All were given short term exemptions from enlisting in the army or navy.

During the war death came in many different guises and for many different reasons, not all of which were the result of a bomb or bullet. Each one had its own sadness. Here's one such story:

Chelmsford Chronicle Friday, 14 April 1916

Hornchurch Tragedy

Found Drowned After Shattered Romance

On Tuesday Mr C Edgar Lewis, Coroner, held an inquest on Lydia

Newman, aged 24, of High Street, Hornchurch, (daughter of Mrs Newman, a widow), whose body was found in the Ingrebourne Brook at Sutton's Farm, Hornchurch, on Saturday.

The deceased was a domestic servant at Westcliff, but just before Christmas she came home to look after her mother. On Saturday morning she said, 'Goodbye, mum; I shall be home soon after half past twelve.'

The mother later heard that she had not gone to the place where she had arranged to go. She also knew that recently she had been keeping company with a man named Geer, who was acting as a cook at Grey Towers Camp, and who lodged with them. They were engaged to be married a week from that date. Geer left their house on the previous Monday week. Since Thursday four letters had been received from Geer in which he referred to a coming Court Martial. He also asked deceased not to worry about him. In one letter he referred to a communication he had received from the deceased, and wrote, 'For Heaven's sake don't think of doing what you say. If anything happens I will put a bullet through my head.'

Letters found at deceased mother's house since Geer left, which he had written but not posted, were produced, and these referred to his wife. Deceased's mother did not know Geer was married until she saw these letters. On Sunday his wife came down to see her.

Millie Geer, 20, Borstal Hill, Plumstead, said she was the wife of William Geer, and had been married to him for eight years (a statement which obviously cannot be correct). They lived together until he joined the Army, about two months before the war broke out. He was an electrical wireman by trade. She had been corresponding with him at Hornchurch. On the previous Friday the deceased came to her father's house at Plumstead, but she did not see her. She left after speaking with her father.

The deceased's body was found by a young lad by the name of Fred Morgan, which at the time was lying face down in the water. There was a chain with a locket around the deceased's neck which contained two photographs, one of which was of the deceased the other was of Geer. There were no injuries found on the body and there were no obvious signs of any struggle having taken place.

Supt. W T J Howlett, from Romford Police station, said that on the previous Tuesday Geer was in custody at the Police station, but initially he had given his name as Dyer. While in custody awaiting an escort he was visited by the deceased. She seemed desperately fond of him and sat with him for a long time. She told the Superintendent that they were to be married in a fortnight.

The article didn't explain the reason why Geer had been arrested which led to him being in custody. There is no sign of his name on the Commonwealth War Graves Commission website, so it would appear that whatever the outcome of the court martial, he survived the war which, sadly, is more than can be said for Lydia Newman, whose only mistake was to fall in love with the wrong man.

Tribunals where men tried to gain exemption certificates from enlisting in the military, were held on Fridays, Saturdays and Mondays. There was an interesting article in the same edition on this topic:

Three Brother Objectors

Ernest Stanley Whiffen, clerk, Romford, said all killing was most revolting, and he could conceive nothing more horrible than a soul going before its maker stained with a fellow man's blood. He believed war was nothing short of murder. He belonged to the Church of England. He was willing to take a position in any office which did no work associated with war if one could be found. He had two other brothers appealing as conscientious objectors.

Harold Livingstone Whiffen, head correspondence clerk, appealing on similar lines, said he had been granted a certificate for non-combatant service, but he believed he was doing his duty better in his present position.

Norman Wilberforce Whiffen, Great Eastern Railway clerk, Romford, said militarism was an organisation for human slaughter. All the railway clerks before the Romford Tribunal had been granted exemption. There was no religion in the Army. The Chairman: 'That is a rather big statement to make.' Appellant: 'It is a big order.' The Chairman: 'The head of your Church has been to the front holding services?' Appellant: 'Yes, as Chaplin.

*If you know any religion in the Army, God help you.' Captain
Howard: 'You would find there is true Christianity in the trenches
if anywhere.' Appellant: 'I am told of hymn tunes they sing, but
the words are the biggest blasphemy.' A Member: 'Have you any
objection to being shot?' Appellant: 'I would rather be shot than
fight for the Army, but I am not particularly anxious to be shot.'
A Member: 'Would you try to protect yourself if the country were
invaded?' Appellant: 'To a certain extent I should.'*

*The Chairman said all three appellants would have to go for
full service. One Appellant: 'They will never have any service out
of me.'*

The following report is about Alfred Unwin, who was 38 years of age
and lived at number 23, Marks Road, Romford, with his parents Walter
and Sophia. It's not known what subsequently happened to Alfred,
whether he was forced to enlist or whether he went to prison for his
beliefs:

Essex Newsman Saturday, 15 April 1916

Local Tribunals

*Reference was made to the case of Alfred Unwin, a boot repairer,
of Mildmay Road, Romford, who at the Romford Police court last
week was summoned for failing to report himself under the
Military Services Act. Before the Justices, Unwin stated that he
thought that was the Court at which he would appeal. He knew
now that he had made a mistake in not appealing to the tribunal.
The Court case was adjourned for a fortnight to allow defendant
to make an appeal at the Tribunal. Applicant now asked the
Tribunal for extra time so that he might appeal. He stated that he
had a conscientious objection to taking any part in the war. It
seemed to him that if men were going into the Army to defend their
principles he had a right to step away and suffer rather than do
what he considered to be wrong.*

Leave to appeal was refused.

No doubt there were many applications for exemption from joining the
army which went before these tribunals that were genuine cases where
families would suffer great hardship if the man of the family should

have to go off and fight. It has to be remembered that Britain wasn't a welfare state at that time. If a person couldn't pay their way, then it was off to the workhouse. Having said that, some of the applications were no doubt nothing more than a blatant attempt at escaping military service, simply because the applicant didn't want to go off and fight.

Essex Newsman Saturday, 6 May 1916

> *Henry Arthur Abraham, stores record clerk, Dagenham, appealed on the ground that he had promised his mother not to join the Army, and that it would be against his conscience to do so. Appellant said fighting was against all Christian principles and teaching. In answer to Captain Howard, appellant admitted that he was employed by a firm engaged in ammunition work. The appeal was .... Dismissed.*

1917

As the war continued through 1916 and into 1917 there were more and more tribunal hearings where men were requesting certificates of exemption from joining the British Armed Forces. The details and outcome of each hearing and the names of those to whom they related were openly reported in the newspapers. If the same were to happen today, solicitors and barristers would be quoting their clients human rights and how the tribunals were breaching them. Back in the First World War there was no such thing as human rights legislation.

Even allowing for wartime restrictions on the press about what they could and couldn't report on, there were still some interesting articles worth reading.

Essex Newsman Saturday, 3 June 1916

Cinema Manager Arrested

> *William Sumner, 32, manager of the Laurie Cinema, Market Place, Romford, of Finsbury Park Road, Stoke Newington, was charged with failing to report himself under the Military Service Act at Romford on March 3. Defendant said he got his exemption papers in June last year, and thought they were sufficient. Detective Constable Hyde said he saw defendant on May 17,*

when he stated that he tried to enlist on June 3 1915, but was rejected as medically unfit. Witness pointed out that did not help him as, under the Military Service Act, it was necessary for men who tried to enlist before August 1915, to report themselves. As defendant explained that his arrest would mean closing the cinema, witness told him that it was essential he should take steps at once, and he promised to do so if allowed a few days. Witness saw him again on May 31 and took him into custody. Sergeant Major G Ostler, of the Stratford Recruiting Staff, said no notice was sent to this man because they were only men who were attested and been grouped who received notice. Under the Military Service Act the proclamation was sufficient for a man like this. Defendant said he was perfectly willing to join and it was only a matter of negligence on his part. He received no notice and was waiting until he received the Army papers.

In answer to the Chairman, he said he would take all necessary steps to join up if time were allowed him. He would go to Warley on Friday. The Chairman said he would be allowed five days. If he had not then taken the necessary steps he would be arrested.

Saturday, 12 August 1916

Personal War Notes

Pt. E W Luke of Upminster received several flesh wounds in the face and shoulder, and a fractured elbow.

The Military Medal has been awarded to Rifleman Reginald Jones, Kings Royal Rifles, for bravery in the field. He is the eldest son of Mr T W Jones of 5 Olive Street, Romford, and was a member of the 3rd Romford Boy Scouts.

Second Lieutenant O E Simmonds, Royal Flying Corps, 18, eldest son of the Rev. F T Simmonds, Congregation minister, Romford, is in Denmark Hill Hospital suffering from the effects of shock following an encounter with the enemy in the air. He was formerly at Brentwood Grammar School.

Driver William Smith, Royal Field Artillery, son of Mr and Mrs J H Smith, Mildmay Road, Romford, has been injured through being thrown from his horse and run over by a gun carriage. The muscles of one of his legs were contracted, and he also sustained internal injuries. He is now in York Hospital and is making satisfactory progress.

Pt. Albert Basil Harrington, son of Mr Edward Harrington, Eastern Road, Romford, is lying in Portsmouth Hospital suffering from wounds in the arms and shoulder, which he received in France. Harrington is attached to the Sportsman's Battalion, which were originally stationed at Grey Towers Camp, Hornchurch. He joined when he was sixteen and a half years of age.

Essex Newsman Saturday, 24 November 1917

'Lt. Herbert James Brown, Royal Welsh Fusiliers, killed in action on 6 November 1916, had his home at Romford where he was well known as a keen cricketer and footballer. He leaves a widow and a little daughter. Deceased was the eldest son of Mr E J Brown of Blackheath. He joined the old Boys Corps in September 1914.

Reading through the newspapers, and as the war progressed into its third year, it was becoming very apparent to everybody that British losses were becoming greater and greater. The regular roll of honours of those killed had begun in the latter part of 1914 and continued throughout 1915, increasing in size as time went by, but in 1916, suddenly entire pages of newspapers were required to record the losses, rather than half a column. During the years of the First World War both daily and weekly newspapers were of the broadsheet variety and not the much smaller size of the daily tabloids which make up most of today's papers.

Essex Newsman Saturday, 2 September 1916

Mr and Mrs W Hitch, of 1 Oak Terrace, Hornchurch Road, Romford, have been informed that their son, Drummer Herbert Percy Hitch of the Essex Regt. (Attached to the Gloucestershire Regiment), has been killed in action. Drummer Hitch was only 18 years of age. He was at camp with the Essex Territorials when war broke out, and had been on active service ever since. His father had been in communication with the War Office with a view to his being sent back until he reached 19. He was an old St

Edwards School boy, and was formerly in St Edwards Church choir.

He has a brother who is serving in Egypt in the Royal Field Artillery. Before he went on active service Drummer Hitch was a clerk in the goods office at the Great Eastern Railway's office at Ilford Railway station.

Herbert Percy Hitch was attached to the 1st/4th Battalion of the Gloucestershire Regiment and was killed in action on 16 August 1916. He is buried in the Pozières British Cemetery at Ovillers-la-Boiselle, in the Somme region of France. His parents, William and Maria, at the time of the 1911 census lived at Priests Yard, Havering Road, Romford, but by the time the Commonwealth War Graves Commission had compiled their records, they had moved on and now lived at number 50, Como Street, Romford. Percy had five brothers, William (Jnr), who at 16 was the oldest of the boys, John, 14, Reginald, 7, and Thomas who was 3 years of age. He also had two sisters, Ethel, who was 17, and baby Ivy, who was seven months old. William initially enlisted into the 2nd Battalion, Essex Battery, Royal Field Artillery, on 17 October 1910 at the age of 17. He was mobilized for war on 5 August 1914. William survived the war, eventually dying in March 1980 at the ripe old age of 85. John does not appear to have served at all during the war. He emigrated to Australia on 11 December 1929.

What was quite noticeable in nearly all of the newspapers during the war was the amount of detail they went in to. They certainly left little out. If there was a meeting they would name the entire list of committee members in attendance. If there was a court case they would go through the entire list of witnesses, recording everything each of them had said. If there was a presentation or an unveiling of a war memorial, not only would they name all of the dignitaries who were present, but they would name all of the hymns or songs that were sung as well.

Chelmsford Chronicle Friday, 29 September 1916

Romford Cadets Battalion

Presentation of Colours

On Saturday, the 4th Cadet Battalion Essex Regiment (Romford District) were presented with the King's Colour. The ceremony was performed by Mrs T Gardner, of Hornchurch, and took place in the presence of a large gathering on Romford Sports Ground. The Battalion, which was strengthened by the Bocking, Braintree and Broomfield Companies, presented a good appearance as they marched to the grounds, headed by the band of the Artists Rifles.

Following an inspection by the numerous amount of high-ranking Army officers in attendance, the colours, as is tradition at such ceremonies, were placed across the drums by 2nd Lieutenant Wackett who was accompanied by two Non Commissioned Officers. The service of consecration was then performed by the Bishop of Barking, after which the hymn, 'O God, our help in ages past,' was sung, the singing being led by the band of the Artists Rifles.

Here is a report of a local soldier who died from illness:

Chelmsford Chronicle Friday, 2 March 1917

Romford – Military Funeral

The funeral took place on Monday, with full military honours, of Sergeant Charles A Samson, 2nd Artists Rifles. Deceased was a native of Jersey, and had been married just over a year, and recently he had resided with his wife at 41 Como Street [Romford]. His death took place on Friday, from heart failure following an illness contracted in France. At Hornchurch Parish Church the funeral service was impressively conducted by the Rev. H B Curtis, C F. The chief mourners included Mrs Samson, widow; Mr and Mrs Samson, father and mother: and other relatives. Eight Sergeants from the Artists Rifles acted as bearers.

There were over a million men who went before tribunals during the war who wanted to be exempt from having to enlist in His Majesty's armed services. Some of these took place at a local level and others took part on a county level at Chelmsford. After the war was over, the Government ordered all local authorities to destroy any documentation that they had in their possession in relation to tribunals. Most authorities complied with the instruction, but thankfully some didn't and it is because of them that some of the relevant documentation relating to tribunals still survives, mainly in local public record offices, there for everybody to see. We will leave you to decide for yourself why you believe the Government wanted all tribunal documentation destroyed.

What was also noticeable from reading through the newspapers was the increase in the cost of food prices in general, as well as an increase in wages. There appeared to be a continuous issue with the price of milk in so far as how much in real terms it was costing farmers to produce, balanced against how much they could sell it for, especially when the cost of having it delivered by train was factored in.

Each area had its own Food Control Committee which had been put in place to ensure that prices of much-needed foodstuffs didn't spiral out of control, in particular milk and meat. It is debatable how successful these committees actually were. Britain was an island nation greatly affected by the German strategy of sinking allied merchant shipping. When these supplies failed to arrive, what was available became more sought-after and valuable which meant they could fetch a much higher price on the open market.

The costs involved in keeping a horse had increased considerably. One hundred years ago the necessity of owning a horse was no different from today's need for most people to own a car. Keeping a horse meant having a stable to keep it in. It needed feeding, shoeing and livery to ride it or to use it for the purpose for which it was owned, such as working on a farm or pulling a cart. Add to this the cost of the horse in the first place, which for a bay was easily in excess of £100 (which converts to over £7,000 today). For car owners now it isn't much different. A stable has become a garage. Food has become petrol or diesel and livery has become insurance, servicing and MOT. Before the war the cost of keeping a horse was on average twelve shillings a week; by the end of 1917 that cost had more than doubled to twenty-five shillings a week.

Wages were another bone of contention. Before the war an average wage for a working man employed say as a farm labourer was on average twenty-three shillings per week. By the latter stages of 1917 that had nearly doubled to £2.

1918

In March 1918 the newspapers showed that the Government were looking at bringing in an updated Military Service Bill. Two of the bill's main points were to drastically redefine the criteria which allowed individuals to be provided with exemption certificates. The article didn't provide precise information on what that actually meant but the inference was that exemptions weren't going to be so easily obtained. The other main point was that the age limit for being 'called up for military service', was almost certainly going to be raised to fifty. The reason that the Government had to take such drastic measures was because of the continuing high numbers of casualties which the army were sustaining each month. Some figures for the five months from November 1917 to March 1918 were as follows (they include those who were both wounded and killed):

> **November 1917.** Officers 4,906. Other ranks 124,896.
> **December 1917.** Officers 3,984. Other Ranks 59,031.
> **January 1918.** Officers 1,484. Other Ranks 72,912.
> **February 1918.** Officers 657. Other Ranks 18,412.
> **March 1918.** Officers 942. Other Ranks 10,626.

The above figures were issued by the War Office and show a total of 297,850 casualties which equates to nearly 60,000 per week. The figures for March were incomplete; in the same month there was also a total of 411 officers and other ranks recorded as missing. This normally meant they had been taken prisoner, lost in a water-filled shell hole, or simply blown to pieces. It is no wonder the Government needed more and more men to enlist.

Here is the story of a Romford man who escaped from captivity:

Liverpool Daily Post Saturday, 18 May 1918

Escape from German Camp

Lieutenant P F Dale, Essex Regiment, eldest son of the Rev. Herbert Dale, Rector of Hornchurch, near Romford has just reached his home, having escaped from the prisoners of war camp at Ludwigshafen, in Germany, where he had been confined for two years and seven months. He was captured in the attack on Loos on September 26, 1915, and had, before finally winning his way to freedom, made four previous attempts to escape.

Sadly, five months later in October 1918, Reverend Hale passed away, by which time his son Lieutenant Philip Hale was once again on active service in France. Reverend Hale was 70 years of age and had been in ill health for some years. He had retired only a matter of weeks before his death.

There was an interesting article in the same newspaper concerning body armour, then called 'body shields':

Body Shields for Soldiers

Mr Leslie Scott has put down a question to the Under-Secretary of State for War whether he is aware that the Chemico Body Shield, when worn by soldiers, has successfully resisted both bullets and shrapnel and already saved many lives which otherwise would have certainly been lost; whether if it were included in the regulation outfit of officers and men a very large number of casualties would be avoided; and whether the Government will, therefore, take steps to have it put into universal and immediate use.

Little did Mr Scott know that many years would pass and another world war before the Government would go down the road of supplying its officers and men with body armour while engaged on active service in a war zone.

Just as the war was coming to its end, the flu epidemic arrived with a vengeance. In the first week of November 1918 there were a total of 7,412 flu-related deaths throughout England and Wales. It was no respecter of age or social position; old and young alike were falling victim to its spreading tentacles of death, no one was safe.

CHAPTER 18

St Edward the Confessor Church Romford – Roll of Honour

The St Edward the Confessor Church is located in the Romford Market area. Inside, and adorning one of its fabled walls, are two large ornately carved wooden plaques which commemorate the names of 262 men from Romford who went off to fight in the First World War and never came back. Most of these names are also recorded on the main Romford War Memorial.

Rather than retype the names out I thought it would be better to include photographs of the two plaques so that they could be seen in their true splendour.

It is remarkable to think that the cost of the plaques was paid for out of collections gathered from local parishioners and other townsfolk at a time when money was not plentiful.

(Photograph Sean Connolly)

(Photograph Sean Connolly)

CHAPTER 19

Hornchurch Aerodrome – Sutton's Farm

Hornchurch Aerodrome, or Sutton's Farm as it was also known, played a pivotal role in the First World War by providing the base for aircraft to patrol the skies over Southern England and in so doing to protect and save the lives of hundreds if not thousands of innocent civilians who were harmlessly going about their daily routines. Brave and heroic young men of the embryonic Royal Flying Corps risked their lives every time they were called upon to take to the skies and fly a sortie against their German enemy. Many of these young men inadvertently made a name for themselves amongst an adoring public with their acts of derring do. Some died a hero's death or etched out a place in history ensuring they were remembered and revered for evermore. Although all of them were unquestionably brave, only a few achieved fame, and only a few received awards for gallantry. In the following pages we will look at just a few of these young men who flew out of Sutton's Farm.

Wulstan Joseph **Tempest** was born in Ackworth, Yorkshire, on 22 January 1890 and at the outbreak of war joined the 6th Battalion, Kings Own Yorkshire Light Infantry, as a lieutenant. He was wounded at the first Battle of Ypres and returned home to England to recover from his injuries during which time he decided to try his luck at being a pilot. He attended the Military Flying School at Ruislip where he completed and passed the course in a Maurice Farman Biplane. He was awarded his pilot's certificate on 22 May 1916 after which he was posted to

Sutton's Farm, Hornchurch, as part the Royal Flying Corps 39 Home Defence Squadron, who spent their time flying night patrols over southern England. His claim to fame came on the evening of 1/2 October 1916 when he was credited with shooting down the German Zeppelin *L31* which crashed at Potters Bar in Hertfordshire killing all of the crew. On returning to his base at Sutton's Farm after carrying out his heroics, he had the embarrassment of crash-landing his plane; but thankfully he was not seriously injured. For his actions that evening, Tempest was awarded a much merited Distinguished Service Order.

At the outbreak of the war, Frederick **Sowrey** was completing his graduate studies, but soon after war was declared, he volunteered for military service, on 31 August 1914, and was commissioned as a second lieutenant in the Royal Fusiliers. He was wounded at the Battle of Loos in France in October 1915 and sent home to have his wounds tended and to recuperate. After three months in hospital it was decided that he was no longer fit for military service and was invalided out of the army. Rather than take the easy option and return to his studies, he wasted no time and joined the Royal Flying Corps in late December 1915. After completing his basic aeronautical training, he was posted to Sutton's Farm. He arrived there on 17 June 1916. It would be more than three months before he would achieve his first confirmed enemy 'kill', but it was worth waiting for and one that would ensure his place in history. On the evening of 23 September 1916, he flew off into the night sky over the Essex countryside in a Royal Aircraft Factory B.E.2, which was a single engine, two seater biplane, a type which had been in service with the Royal Flying Corps from 1912. He was flying at about 13,000 feet and had been on patrol for about one and a half hours when he first spotted what would turn out to be the Zeppelin *L32*. The German airship had been on a bombing mission to London and was now on its way home. It was ten past one in the early hours of the morning of 24 September when, despite the difficulties of single-handedly engaging a much larger enemy aircraft, Sowrey decided that the best form of defence was attack, and he proceeded to fire three drums of incendiary ammunition into the belly of the airship causing it to burst into flames. It crashed into the ground at Great Burstead just outside Billericay. All of the crew on board perished with every one of them, bar the captain, who had jumped to his death, burning in the wreckage. For his gallant actions that night Lieutenant Frederick Sowrey was awarded the Distinguished Service Order. On 23 November 1917 Sowrey was awarded the Military Cross. The citation for the award as reported in the *London Gazette* on 6 April 1918, read as follows:

> *For conspicuous gallantry and devotion to duty in shooting down in less than two months, two Albatross Scouts, a Rumpler two-seater, and a Fokker Scout, and in two engagements flying very low and engaging and scattering hostile enemy.*

He was also awarded the Air Force Cross on 1 January 1919.

William Leefe Robinson VC, Wulstan J. Tempest DSO MC and Frederick Sowrey DSO MC AFC.

Photo, *Sports and General Agency.*   THE ZEPPELIN DESTROYERS :
Captain W. L. Robinson, V.C., Lieut. W. J. Tempest, D.S.O., and Lieut. Frederick Sowrey, D.S.O.

William Leefe **Robinson** was born on 14 July 1895 in Coorg, India on his father's coffee estate. Just after the First World War had begun, in August 1914, Robinson entered the Royal Military Academy at Sandhurst. On completing his training, in December 1915, he joined the Worcestershire Regiment as a second lieutenant. In March the following year, having decided he wanted to be a pilot, he transferred to the Royal Flying Corps and went to serve in France as an observer. Despite being wounded while flying over Lille, he wasn't deterred from a military career that saw him in the air rather than on land or sea. He returned to Great Britain where he completed his pilot training and was then attached to number 39, Home Defence Squadron, which was a night flying sorties from Sutton's Farm. His opportunity to make a name for himself came on the night of 2/3 September 1916 while flying over Cuffley, Hertfordshire in a converted B.E.2c night fighter. Although he didn't know it at the time, the Zeppelin which would change Robinson's life for ever had, along with fifteen other Zeppelins, already left her base in Germany for a large-scale bombing raid on southern England. The airship which would end up defining Robinson was *SL11*. It would gain him fame and wealth the likes of which most people could only dream about. On spotting it he knew what he had to do. It was just him against the airship. In those days there was no radio on his aircraft to call for assistance. All he had was his skill as a pilot and his machine guns to win the day. So it was that at 11,500 feet he attacked, coming in from below the Zeppelin, opening fire as he closed in on his target, raking the airship with his guns. At first it looked like his attack had been ineffective, so he flew past and manoeuvred himself into position ready to strike at his enemy once again. Before he could continue the attack the *SL11* suddenly burst in to flames. It crashed in a field at the rear of the Plough Inn, Cuffley in Hertfordshire. All sixteen of the Zeppelin's crew were killed. For his actions that night William Leefe Robinson was awarded the Victoria Cross which was presented to him by King George V at Windsor Castle. Such was the upsurge of national fervour at his heroic deeds that a national collection was held that raised £3,500, a staggering amount of money in 1916, which was handed to Robinson. The people of Hornchurch, where he was based, also presented him with a silver cup to commemorate his deed. Soon afterwards Robinson wrote the following memo to his commanding officer, which is included in the Wikipedia entry for William Leefe Robinson:

September 1916

From: Lieutenant Leefe Robinson, Sutton's Farm.

To: The Officer Commanding No. 39 H D Squadron.

Sir:

I have the honour to make the following report on night patrol made by me on the night of 2/3 instant. I went up at about 11.08 pm on the night of the second with instructions to patrol between Sutton's Farm and Joyce Green.

I climbed to 10,000 feet in fifty-three minutes. I counted what I thought were ten sets of flares – there were a few clouds below me, but on the whole it was a beautifully clear night. I saw nothing until 1.10 am, when two searchlights picked up a Zeppelin S E of Woolwich. The clouds had collected in this quarter and the searchlights had some difficulty in keeping on the airship.

By this time I had managed to climb to 12,000 feet and I made in the direction of the Zeppelin – which was being fired on by a few anti-aircraft guns – hoping to cut it off on its way eastward. I very slowly gained on it for about ten minutes.

I judged it to be about 800 feet below me and I sacrificed some speed in order to keep the height. It went behind some clouds, avoiding the searchlight, and I lost sight of it. After fifteen minutes of fruitless search I returned to my patrol.

I managed to pick up and distinguish my flares again. At about 1.50 am I noticed a red glow in the N E of London. Taking it to be an outbreak of fire, I went in that direction. At 2.05 a Zeppelin was picked up by the searchlights over NNE London (As far as I could judge).

Remembering my last failure, I sacrificed height (I was at about 12,900 feet) for speed and nosed down in direction of the Zeppelin. I saw shells bursting and night tracers flying around it.

When I drew closer I noticed that the anti-aircraft aim was too high or too low; also a good many shells burst about 800 feet behind – a few tracers went right over. I could hear the bursts when about 3,000 feet from the Zeppelin.

I flew about 800 feet below it from bow to stern and distributed one drum among it (alternate New Brock and Pomeroy). It seemed to have no effect.

I therefore moved to one side and gave them another drum along the side – also without effect. I then got behind it and by this time I was very close – 500 feet or less below, and concentrated one drum on one part (underneath rear). I was then at a height of 11,500 feet when attacking the Zeppelin. I had hardly finished the drum before I saw the part fired at, glow. In a few seconds the whole rear part was blazing. When the third drum was fired, there were no search lights on the Zeppelin, and no anti-aircraft was firing.

I quickly got out of the way of the falling, blazing Zeppelin and, being very excited, fired off a few red Very lights and dropped a parachute flare.

Having little oil or petrol left, I returned to Sutton's Farm, landing at 2.45 am. On landing I found the Zeppelin gunners had shot away the machine-gun wire guard, the rear part of my centre section, and had pierced the main spar several times.

I have the honour to be, sir,

Your obedient servant

(Signed)

W. Leefe Robinson, Lieutenant

No 39 Squadron, R F C.

Below is a post card issued at the time to commemorate William Leefe Robinson's achievement of shooting down the German Zeppelin *SL11* and having been awarded the Victoria Cross for his actions in September 1916:

Lieut. William Leefe Robinson, V.C.

Excerpt from the ''London Gazette.''

Lieut. **William Leefe Robinson, V.C.**
Worcester Regiment and R.F.C.

For most conspicuous bravery. He attacked an enemy airship under circumstances of great difficulty and danger, and sent it crashing to the ground as a flaming wreck.

He had been in the air for more than two hours and had previously attacked another airship during his flight.

Once the excitement, hype, and the public appearances had finished, it was back to work for Robinson, in April 1917, when he was posted to France as a flight commander with No. 48 Squadron of the Royal Flying Corps, which had originally been formed on 15 April 1916 at Netheravon in Wiltshire. The Squadron had been equipped with the then new Bristol F.2 Fighter two-seater biplane. On his very first patrol since having arrived in France, Robinson was in a six-aircraft formation on 5 April 1917 when they encountered a group of German fighters led by the renowned German fighter pilot Manfred von Richthofen, who was also known as the Red Baron. In the ensuing skirmish four of the British planes were shot down including that of Robinson who was wounded and taken prisoner. The German pilot who shot Robinson down was Sebastian Festner, a *Vizefeldwebel*, the equivalent in rank in either the British army or RFC/RFA to that of sergeant, who was also shot down and killed just twenty days later on 25 April 1917. By all accounts Robinson was not well treated by his German captors, possibly because of his shooting down of the Zeppelin *SL11*. He was held at both Zorndorf and Holzminden PoW camps in Germany from where he attempted to escape on several occasions, which resulted in him been held in solitary confinement at Holzminden. He remained in captivity until the end of the war, returning to England in early December. He died at the home of his sister, the Baroness Heyking, on 18 December 1918, at Stanmore in Middlesex after having contracted influenza. He is buried at Harrow Weald in the churchyard at All Saints Church.

William Leefe Robinson's headstone. **(Wikipedia)**

William Leefe Robinson's Victoria Cross sold at auction at Christie's in London on Tuesday, 22 November 1988, for £99,000. It was sold by Robinson's niece Mrs Regina G. Libin with the proceeds going to a charitable trust set up to benefit children who were suffering from leukaemia.

Although the most universally well-known pilot associated with Sutton's Farm in Hornchurch is undoubtedly William Leefe Robinson VC, the most highly-decorated pilot to have flown out of the air base was Major James Thomas Byford **McCudden** VC DSO & Bar MC & Bar MM Croix de Guerre.

McCudden was born in Gillingham on 28 March 1895 into a middle class working family with strong military traditions. From these beginnings he would go on to become one of the most highly decorated pilots in British military history. It is recorded that McCudden enlisted in the Royal Engineers in 1910. If true, this means he would have been only 15 years of age. He transferred to the Royal Flying Corps in 1913 where he became an observer, not obtaining his pilot's licence until 1916. When he first arrived in France with 3 Squadron in August 1914 he was there only as a mechanic, but soon McCudden was being used as an observer on reconnaissance missions. He won the first of his gallantry awards on 21 January 1916 when he was awarded the Croix de Guerre for gallantry by French General, Joseph Joffre, Commander-in-Chief of the French army. Previous attempts to be allowed to train to be a pilot had been denied him because his skills as a mechanic were much needed, but after being awarded this medal he was allowed to return to England to commence training and realize his dream of becoming a pilot. After successfully completing his course and qualifying as a pilot, he returned to France on 8 July 1916 and joined 20 Squadron. He claimed his first victory in September 1916 and his fifth in February of the following year, officially making him an ace. These actions won him both the Military Medal and the Military Cross. He returned to England in February 1917 when he served with 66 Squadron, which at the time was flying Sopwith Pup aircraft. The squadron was based at Sutton's Farm. As his number of kills increased, so did his count of gallantry awards. On 6 October 1917 he was awarded a bar to his Military Cross. Two months later he was awarded a DSO and Bar, and on 30 March 1918 he was awarded his VC. He

would go on to make a total of 57 confirmed victories, 31 of which came in the last six months of 1917. He was killed in a flying accident on 9 July 1918 in France when his aircraft crashed following engine failure soon after take-off from Auxi-le-Château in his SE5a. The normal procedure in such a situation was to glide directly to a forced landing, but instead McCudden decided to try to turn around and return to his base. His aircraft stalled on the turn and he crashed. He died

James McCudden's grave.
(Wikipedia)

of his wounds two hours later in hospital. He was 23 years of age. The night before his death he had stayed with his family in Tunbridge Wells. The following morning, before taking off for France, he handed his sister an envelope over breakfast which contained all of his medals. Maybe it was just for safekeeping or maybe he had a premonition, we shall never know for sure. McCudden was buried at the Wavans British Cemetery in the Pas-de-Calais.

CHAPTER 20

Romford's Women in the Great War

Women played an important role in the war effort, not by fighting at the side of their men in the trenches of France, but on the home front back in England. To a large extent it was largely down to them that society stayed on an even keel. They kept the wheels of industry and commerce turning so that everyday life for the general public could continue as smoothly as it could in the circumstances.

Women up and down the country answered the 'call to arms'. Women from Romford, Upminster and Hornchurch were no different, for everywhere was the same. Prior to the war, women had been restricted in what they could do in the workplace. For most, the only occupations available were nursing, shop work or domestic service. These were the roles which the unwritten rules of society deemed were suitable for women, other than being a wife, a mother and a home maker. But during the First World War, this began to change.

It wasn't only paid work that was involved; women were volunteering for unpaid jobs which would make soldiers' lives better. In the early days of the war, this was mostly unorganized and uncoordinated.

As the war continued and the need for more and more men to go off and fight kept increasing, so did the call on women to do more and more on the home front. Jobs which had hitherto been the sole domain of men were now becoming commonplace for the fairer sex. Women were now literally wearing the trousers, while they delivered the mail, drove buses, collected bus tickets or drove taxis.

Not surprisingly during a time of war munitions factories were suddenly popping up all over the place. They needed people to work in them and in most cases that meant women. Some of them died working in these factories, not because of explosions (although these did occur from time to time) or from air raids, but from illnesses which they contracted through handling the various munitions and the components which were used in their making. The jobs which women workers in Britain's munitions factories undertook was fundamental to the success of the war effort.

Numerous official organizations for women came into being as a direct result of the war, most of which were known more readily by the acronyms which were used to abbreviate them. There were VADs, the WAAC, the WRNS, the WRAF, and the Women's Land Army.

Volunteer Aid Detachments, to give them their full title, included both men and women, although most sections were predominantly made up of the latter. It was a joint venture between the British Red Cross and the Order of St John, its purpose being to have a volunteer group of people who could effectively support and assist the work of nursing in general. They were taught basic first aid and given tuition in other matters such as making beds and providing bed baths for wounded and sick soldiers, as well as working as admin clerks, telephone operators and X-ray attendants.

VADs weren't solely used on the home front; many volunteered to work overseas in France, Belgium and other theatres of war, working in field hospitals, casualty clearing stations, or as ambulance drivers, all of the roles placing them in great danger. Many VADs were either wounded or killed by enemy fire, especially in the latter stages of the war when German artillery bombardments became more indiscriminate in their targeting of British and allied military positions.

The main objective of the Women's Army Auxiliary Corps was to undertake certain roles in the army which had previously been carried out by soldiers so that more men could be released for service at the front to fight.

During the First World War when the 2nd Battalion, the Artists Rifles, were in barracks at the Hare Hall Army camp in Romford, they had a section of WAACs attached to them, probably engaged in either admin type work or the cooking of meals for the soldiers.

WAACs did not come into existence until very late on in the war in 1917. Recruiting began in March 1917, but the order which formally established the Women's Auxiliary Army Corps wasn't actually issued until 7 July 1917 and their first Chief Officer was Mrs Chalmers-Watson.

Although it was an official, uniformed service the WAACs, it has been claimed, had no rank structure. Instead it was made up of 'officials' and 'members', but with the latter being subordinate to the officials. The WAACs were divided into four separate sections, which dealt with the areas of cooking, mechanical and clerical, with anything outside these areas coming into the category of what was described as miscellaneous.

In appreciation of its good work, the WAAC were renamed the Queen Mary Auxiliary Army Corps on 9 April 1918, with its new commander-in-chief becoming none other than Her Majesty the Queen. During the course of the war some 57,000 women from all over the country and from all walks of life served in the WAACs and the QMAACs. By 1 May 1920 they had ceased to exist.

These organizations were just some of the better known ones. Others included the Women's Legion which focused its work on vehicle mechanics and the driving of motor vehicles. Another was the Navy and Army Canteen Board which, it won't come as a surprise to know, catered for canteens in military establishments up and down the country, of which there were many. There were numerous organizations which provided either nurses or nursing support for both civilian and military hospitals, which included the many convalescent homes for wounded and sick soldiers.

Here are just a few of the local establishments that relied heavily on women workers to carry out the bulk of their work for them during the war:

The VAD hospital at Marshalls Park in Romford. The YMCA at the Grey Towers camp in Hornchurch, when it had become a hospital for recuperating New Zealand Troops. Hare Hall Army Camp at Romford, which at different times was home to both the Artist Rifles and the 2nd Sportsman's Battalion. The delivery of the post throughout the Hornchurch area. Answering the phones at Sutton's Farm RFC/RAF Aerodrome. Over 300 women worked at the Roneo Vickers munitions factory in Romford, where bullets and artillery shells were made throughout the war. Working as a motorcyclist or driving other types of motor vehicles for the Women's Royal Air Force at Sutton's Farm Aerodrome in Hornchurch.

EVERY FIT WOMAN
CAN RELEASE A FIT MAN
JOIN THE
WOMEN'S ARMY
AUXILIARY CORPS
TO-DAY
FOR WORK WITH THE FORCES EITHER AT HOME OR ABROAD
FOR ALL INFORMATION & ADVICE WRITE TO OR APPLY AT
NEAREST EMPLOYMENT EXCHANGE
THE ADDRESS CAN BE OBTAINED WITHIN

Women's Auxiliary Army Corps Poster. **(Bing Images)**

Part of the push to encourage women to 'join up' and become WAACs was done via posters such as the example above, with the message of getting everyone to unite behind the nation's flag and the common cause of doing one's bit for the war effort.

The Women's Royal Naval Service was very similar in its design to that of the WAACs. Its main purpose was to undertake work and roles at ports which had previously been carried out by naval ratings, and in doing so release more men for the war effort. The work was entirely shore-based with women enrolling for a minimum twelve months or the duration of the war, which ever was the longest. With the war eventually lasting for four years and three months that would turn out to be a long year.

As with their male counterparts, the WRNS were either ratings or officers, the latter being expected to undertake the work of either a secretary or the more exciting role of intelligence code breaker. They came into existence even later in the war than the WAACs did, in February 1918.

Late in the war the Royal Air Force was formed from a combination of the Royal Flying Corps and the Royal Navy. They too had a female contingent in the shape of the Women's Royal Air Force. The work which

WAACs recruiting in Trafalgar Square. **(Bing Images)**

they carried out was also varied and included working as wireless operators, fitters and motorcyclists.

The Women's Land Army was different from all of the other female services as it didn't release men who were already in service to go and fight, it did however allow men who had previously been exempt from having to undertake military service because of their employment in agriculture to be called up. Understandably in some cases this led to incidents of resentment towards members of the Women's Land Army from the men who they were replacing and their families.

CHAPTER 21

Romford & District Essex Volunteer Regiment

Local Volunteer Regiments were made up of well-meaning individuals of all different ages, some of who were either too old or too young, or those deemed unfit for wartime military service. As well as doing a useful job, it also provided these men with a feeling of wellbeing and a sense that they were doing their duty. Some were old soldiers who had seen service with the colours back in the latter years of the nineteenth century in places such as India and South Africa, and now wanted the chance to fight for their king and country once again should there be a German invasion.

From very early on in the war nearly every village, town and city across the nation had groups of volunteers springing up all over the place, with men of the Romford, Upminster and Hornchurch areas being no different. The Romford & District Company of the 3rd Essex Volunteer Regiment were for most of the war under the command of Captain C.H. Allen and were inspected on more than one occasion at the town's Artillery Drill Hall which was their home base. Three other officers who were also ever-present with the company throughout most of the war were Lieutenants C.L. Brabant, P.M. Gunn and C.W. Packer. The company quartermaster sergeant was a Mr Daniels.

They were well versed in drill, bayonet and musketry work, as well as bomb-throwing. This was similar instruction to that which was provided for regular soldiers in training for the front. They had uniforms and equipment even down to their own insignia on cap badges.

The Volunteer Training Corps became an extremely useful organization for both home defence efforts, as well as providing experience for young men of what real military life would be like. To this end, men who were below the legal age to enlist in the regular army were allowed to join the volunteers so they could experience and benefit from the training and discipline which they received when they reached the age of 18 and went off to war. Many Volunteers would subsequently join the regular army before the war's end with some of these paying the ultimate price.

CHAPTER 22

Romford's Suspicious Persons

During time of war, it is not unusual for a certain amount of paranoia to set in on the home front. Everybody is encouraged to report anything suspicious to the authorities, no matter how insignificant it might at first appear. The First World War was no different, with people contacting the police almost on a daily basis reporting a friend, relative or somebody who they worked with of acting in a manner that could possibly constitute a threat to national security.

Some of the reports were made in the genuine belief that an individual was up to no good, but some of them were also vexatious. Some allegations were based on nothing more than someone believing that another individual had a German-sounding name.

Every one of these reports had to be recorded and investigated by the police or military intelligence, depending on the agency to which the report had been sent. The names of the people who contacted the authorities filing these reports, or the outcomes of the investigations, have mostly not been recorded. But those that have survived make for interesting, as well as somewhat humorous, reading.

In Essex, all of these reports were handwritten and were contained within a bound book that is entitled *War Suspects*. It details accounts of investigations of those with German associations or with believed German sympathies. The book is held at the Essex Record Office in Chelmsford and originated from Essex County Constabulary.

The first one we looked at comes in to the 'beggars belief' category. G.O. Oglethorpe was a soldier, a private in 'S' Company, 23rd Battalion of the Royal Fusiliers, and was stationed at Grey Towers

Barracks in Hornchurch. The report even included the fact that he could be found in Hut 32 of the barracks.

A Private in the 23rd (S) Battalion, Royal Fusiliers, stationed at Hornchurch. Who while on sick leave stayed at the Montagu Temperance Hotel, 2 Montagu Street, WC, and as he stayed out each night till 1am caused the occupier to suspect him of being a German.

Enquiries were made by both Police and Military, and they were quite satisfied that there was nothing whatever suspicious about him. His birth certificate was obtained and every enquiry respecting him was very satisfactory.

The report doesn't include a date or what ailment had resulted in the soldier being on sick leave or how long he stayed at the hotel. Here we have a serving soldier in the British army during wartime. Whether he had already served abroad and had been involved in some of the fighting isn't clarified. While staying in London on sick leave he decides to stay out late and enjoy himself not knowing when or if he will be able to enjoy such an indulgence again and this results in the owner of the hotel believing he was a German. How that conclusion was arrived at is a mystery in itself.

The second and last report we are going to look at has no connection to the Romford or Hornchurch areas but we decided to include it purely to highlight just how bad the paranoia had become in relation to who was or wasn't a German spy.

The individual concerned in this report was a Mrs Longmuir from Basildon. It is the last line which puts the topic of ordinary members of the public possibly being German spies into context. It read as follows:

On 18th November 1914 an anonymous letter is received through the Metropolitan Police, alleging that Mrs Longmuir was keeping two German boys in her house and was driving her motor car about amongst the troops daily.

Enquiries were made by the Police on 23rd November 1914 who reported having interviewed Mrs Longmuir who resides with her husband at Summerhill, Basildon. She is a member of the relief committee of the district and during the last 10 days has only on one occasion driven her car to Billericay. She denies the allegation of her having German boys in her house. She has taken her son for a drive in the car and on one occasion when returning from Billericay gave two men a lift in her car.

Mrs Longmuir is a very respectable person well known to the Justices at Billericay and is certainly above harbouring German aliens.

Mr Longmuir is a friend of Lord Kitchener.

VAD Nurses and wounded Essex soldiers.

CHAPTER 23

Romford's Voluntary Aid Detachment

Voluntary Aid Detachments, or VADs for short, came into existence, it would be fair to say, as a result of the experience of the Boer War. The War Office were seriously concerned that in the event of another war there wouldn't be enough nurses available to tend to the sick and needy amongst the civilian population, as well as dealing with the large numbers of anticipated wounded and dying soldiers from the battlefield. Not only would numbers increase greatly from what they would be in peacetime, but their medical requirements would be totally different. Instead of the odd broken bone or minor illness there would be gunshot wounds, shrapnel wounds, and the need for amputations. In the event there was also 'shell shock' which hadn't even been thought about at the start of the First World War, but as the years went on would end up requiring entire hospitals to deal with it.

Voluntary Aid Detachments came into being on 16 August 1909 as a direct result of a scheme set up by the War Office. Little did they know that it would be five years to the day when they would be needed for real. During those five years, although it was a really good idea, some found it hard to fully commit to something that they might never actually be called upon to do.

Each detachment varied in size according to the size of the area they covered, but the template for a detachment was a commandant and at least twenty-two women, two of which had to be trained nurses. The idea was that in a time of war VADs, who it was intended would not be sent abroad, would work in auxiliary hospitals and convalescent homes which would allow qualified nurses to be able to focus on their nursing, while they carried out the more subsidiary matters such as changing beds, cleaning the wards, cooking meals, lighting fires or doing the washing.

Although a role predominantly undertaken by women, there were also male VADs as well who were employed as, for example, stretcher bearers or ambulance drivers, and who would pick up wounded soldiers from railway stations and convey them to hospital for treatment.

The training of the VADs was undertaken by a combination of the British Red Cross Society and the Order of St John. Before the start of the First World War there were somewhere in the region of 50,000 VADs and by the end of the war it was estimated that up to double that amount of women had served as VADs.

The Romford VAD consisted of two detachments of women and one of men. The two female units had the official titles of Essex 108 and Essex 110. They had separate commandants: Miss F.B. Bardsley was in charge of 108 and Mrs Walter Frost was in charge of 110. How many women were in each of its detachments is not known.

Mrs Walter Frost is believed to be Edith Rose Frost who was the wife of Walter Frost, an affluent local timber merchant. They lived with their young son Richard at 67 Western Road, Romford. Walter's line of work paid well enough to afford two servants. One was a cook and the other a nurse for Richard and general housemaid.

The male detachment of the VAD was Essex 51 and had Mr Charles A. Newitt as its commandant. It had forty-two men working in the unit at its peak who were used as ambulance drivers. They were orderlies at Marshalls Park Convalescent Home in Romford throughout the war. They stood to arms when notice of Zeppelin raids were announced. They attended thirty-two parades, as well as taking first aid classes which culminated in both written and practical examinations in preparation for the war.

References

British Newspaper Archive

Commonwealth War Grave Commission

National Archive

1914-1918.net

ancestry.co.uk

irishgolfarchive.com

lermuseum.org

queensroyalsurreys.org.uk

wikipedia.com

Index